MW00389143

Praise for *Sacred Trust*

Congressman Hice's journey from a small Baptist parish to the epicenter of the 2020 presidential elections is one of the most riveting and inspiring stories in recent congressional history. Hice did not have the privilege of buying or networking his way into international politics. Like all great Americans, Hice did not covet leadership. The critical role he played in our 2020 elections was not for fame or an enhanced platform. He simply did what he thought was right and let God handle the rest. . . . What I admire so much about the thesis of this book is that Congressman Hice looks beyond partisanship. Instead of focusing on the miasma of our current electoral system, it looks at the greater principles that underline it. . . . Ronald Reagan once said, "The right to vote is the crown jewel of American liberties." Though tragically few Americans utilize their right to participate in this process, it nonetheless remains their most valuable tool. The right to vote is as sacred to the American system of government as the sacrament is to the church. That sacred trust and our electoral system must be guarded at all costs. Doing so will require clear leadership and a road map toward rehabilitating our system. Thankfully, Congressman Jody Hice has given us just that.

—**Ken Blackwell**, bestselling author and Senior Fellow
for Human Rights and Constitutional Governance,
Family Research Council

Former Congressman Jody Hice is a courageous conservative warrior and a true patriot who loves his country. He has been on the front line in the battle for the integrity and security of our elections, as he recognizes that they are vital to the future of America. His insight gained from his experience, and his self-sacrifice in pursuit of a just cause, is informative and inspirational.

    —U.S. **Representative Bob Good**, Virginia's 5th District,
    House Freedom Caucus Chairman

It is critical that the American people have confidence in the integrity of our elections. The Constitution clearly grants the authority and control of elections to the states. I have worked with Jody in Congress to ensure the federal government does not exceed its authority in tampering with elections and appreciate his efforts to share this message with the American people.

    —U.S. **Representative Matt Rosendale**, Montana's 2nd
    District

America has a process by which she handles her business and settles disagreements: the electoral process. If Americans mistrust the sanctity and fidelity of our elections, they either will seek alternative methods of settling those disagreements or disengage altogether. Without the guarantee of integrity and accuracy—at the outset—we have no remedy for a questionable election. It is absolutely critical that our elections remain sacrosanct—completely transparent, failsafe, and above reproach.

    —U.S. **Representative Scott Perry**, Pennsylvania 10th
    District, former House Freedom Caucus Chairman

Election integrity is one of the key pillars that our electoral system is built on. If we don't defend the integrity and justice of our system, then people will lose faith in it. Congressman Hice sheds light on a critical issue facing our nation and provides an excellent blueprint for how we can move forward. This is essential reading for any American who believes in defending our sacred intuitions.

—**U.S. Representative, Andy Biggs**, Arizona's 5th
District, former House Freedom Caucus Chairman

Sacred Trust is essential reading for any patriot looking to right the ship of American integrity. At every corner, our nation is under siege by the Left. Those progressives are devoted to one end: the destruction of our sacred American foundations. Their long march through our nation's institutions has brought us to this decisive moment that will determine the very future of our nation. This book provides essential insight as to how we, as Patriots and as Christians, can stand together and turn back the scourge of the Left.

—**Tony Perkins**, President, Family Research Council

Congressman Jody Hice is one of the most important Christian voices in American politics. Throughout his career, he stood for integrity, liberty, and freedom, especially when it was politically inconvenient. His journey from leading congregations to being a leader in Congress is an inspiration to all. Along the way, he fought with honor and refused to compromise his values, even in the face of staunch opposition. That commitment makes him one of the most important and respected voices in the conservative movement to this day.

—**Dr. Jim Garlow**, CEO, Well Versed

Congressman Jody Hice has dedicated his life to our constitutional freedoms and the fight for conservative values. Over the past few years, he led the charge in exposing the corruption of the electoral system, and Sacred Heart is a glimpse into the systemic problems our great nation faces and how we should address them to secure a better future from the ballot box and beyond.

    —**Jenn Pellegrino**, Newsmax anchor and
    former White House Correspondent

SACRED
TRUST

SACRED TRUST

Election Integrity and the Will of the People

JODY HICE

Humanix Books
www.humanixbooks.com

Humanix Books
Sacred Trust
Copyright © 2024 by Humanix Books

Humanix Books is a division of Humanix Publishing, LLC. Its trademark,
consisting of the words "Humanix Books," is registered in the United States
Patent and Trademark Office and in other countries.

Cover photo © ZUMA Press, Inc./Alamy Live News

ISBN: 978-1-63006-274-3 (Hardcover)
ISBN: 978-1-63006-275-0 (E-book)

Printed in the United States of America
10 9 8 7 6 5 4 3 2 1

This book is dedicated to my precious wife, Dee Dee. Over 40 years ago, you became my bride. Thank you for standing with me day by day, year by year. Through the endless challenges associated with life on the "tip of the spear," you have been my rock and the reason that "home" has always been my favorite place. Thank you for the love, prayers, and inconceivable sacrifices you have made. Thank you for your contagious smile and laughter and for making our home a sanctuary of divine safety and harmony. Thank you for always exhibiting grace, joy, and peace. You are my gift from God, and I cannot say it enough: I love you!

Contents

Foreword

EVERY FOUR YEARS, AMERICA holds a national revolution. Though it's not often thought of that way, that's precisely what voting is. It is the American people utilizing their natural, unalienable right to control and determine the destiny of themselves, their families, and their nation. It is the most powerful tool by which every American, from billionaire coastal elites to bushwhacking rural everymen, has an equal voice in who and what defines our future. In so doing, Thomas Jefferson's "tree of liberty" is renewed not "with the blood of patriots and tyrants" but with the power of ideas and intellectualism.

Voting is a sacred, unalienable right. In 2004, l was given the honor of overseeing Ohio's 2004 presidential elections as the chief elections officer. Yet my efforts to ensure Ohio's elections were fair and free were challenged at every turn by activists' intent on eroding every electoral safeguard. After witnessing this firsthand, I decided to dedicate a significant portion of my life to the battle for election integrity.

Thankfully, I've not been alone in this fight. I've been proud to have Congressman Jody Hice as a brother in arms and a dear friend alongside me at the bulwark. Congressman Hice's journey from a small Baptist parish to the epicenter of the 2020 presidential elections is one of the most riveting and inspiring stories in recent congressional history. Hice did not have the privilege of buying or networking his way into international politics. Like all great Americans, Hice did not covet leadership. The critical role he played in our 2020 elections was not for fame or an enhanced platform. He simply did what he thought was right and let God handle the rest.

There have been many books claiming certain elections throughout American history have been stolen. People claim John F. Kennedy's 1960 victory was only due to his father's New England connections. The chaos of early American elections throughout the nineteenth century were rife with fraud. Heck, an entire library could be filled with liberal books claiming that George Bush's 2000 victory over Al Gore was stolen. Of course, to this day, millions of liberals still believe that Donald Trump's 2016 election was only possible because Russian hackers changed voting rolls in his favor.

What I admire so much about the thesis of this book is that Congressman Hice looks beyond partisanship. Instead of focusing on the miasma of our current electoral system, it looks at the greater principles that underline it. The most essential element in every facet of the American system of government is the full faith and trust of the American people. Legislators and government officials are not inherently entitled to that trust. It must be earned every day by keeping the government honest, fair, and transparent.

The 2020 election was one of the most challenging in American history. With a raging pandemic, excessively onerous lockdowns, and a heavily partisan electorate, ensuring a free election was thought to be an almost impossible period to that end. Liberals actively worked to ease voting restrictions. They permitted everything from unsolicited mail-in ballots to unsupervised ballot drop-offs. When any reasonable-minded person questioned the integrity of these decisions, liberals rolled their eyes. They reassured Americans that these measures were only temporary and necessary precautions in the face of Covid-19.

Years later, the majority of those relaxed electoral standards are still in place. What was billed as onetime, short-term solutions quickly became the standard operating procedure for elections held in liberal counties. Any challenge to their lack of electoral policies was labeled racist, fascist, and un-American. When Governor Ron DeSantis of Florida passed comprehensive electoral reforms, they accused him of stealing democracy from the American people. Yet voting participation increased, and overall satisfaction with the electoral process along with it. Nevertheless, many liberals still seek to undo the positive changes he made.

For years, there has been a shadow campaign to undermine the integrity of our electoral system. By this, I don't mean that Democrats believe in illegal voting—of course, not. But what is clear is that they are blindly committed to eradicating all electoral standards in the name of "social justice." This has led them to completely disregard the objective risks and unintended consequences of lax electoral standards. Their intransigence towards electoral integrity reveals how little they understand about what makes elections secure in America.

Progressives don't seem to understand that in a free society, the perception of justice is almost as important as the application of justice. The perception of election integrity is just as important as the application of electoral integrity. When people see piles of unsolicited mail-in ballots sitting in mail rooms unguarded, they question the system. When they see ballot boxes unattended and voting counts suddenly flip, they question the system. None of these instances are proof of wrongdoing in and of themselves, but they do erode the faith and trust of the American people.

Ronald Reagan once said, "The right to vote is the crown jewel of American liberties." Though tragically few Americans utilize their right to participate in this process, it nonetheless remains their most valuable tool. The right to vote is as sacred to the American system of government as the sacrament is to the church. That sacred trust and our electoral system must be guarded at all costs. Doing so will require clear leadership and a road map toward rehabilitating our system. Thankfully, Congressman Jody Hice has given us just that.

Ken Blackwell

Preface

MEET PEOPLE ALMOST EVERY day, and no matter how warmly the conversation begins, countless chats inevitably lead to the serious problems confronting America. Not just "problems" but severe challenges that most of us never could have imagined. So many issues have become dangerously toxic to our national well-being, and now those issues seem to infect every family in one way or another. The conversations include crime, border security, racism, declining military strength, loss of global respect, China, the pandemic, inflation, terrorism, riots, cancel culture, climate change, government intrusion into our lives, the national debt, corruption, education, healthcare, and a host of other issues. Indeed, it is a frightful time in which we are living. Answers are desperately needed to stop, thwart, or even reverse the current national trajectory. It seems like the "magic wand" that once enabled America to solve problems in past days is no longer to be found. The challenges facing our country are abundant, they are real, and they are gradually changing our republic—for the worse.

No doubt, these and a host of other issues rise to the level of enormous concern for the average citizen. Threats against our culture and traditional way of life; those elements that have historically set America apart from every other country in the world now seem to be hanging by a thread. Many Americans can hardly bear to watch the nightly news. It's too emotionally draining to be bombarded with journalists, images, and articles day after day, portraying the seeming demise of all the things that have united us in the past. To make matters worse, there is a movement, a powerful and in-your-face movement, that openly opposes our treasured national uniqueness. They blame America for the world's problems and accuse free-thinking American individuals of conduct, attitudes, and crimes for which they are not guilty. As a result, we are made to feel responsible for all things wrong in society when, in fact, most of us are simply trying to live our daily lives and raise our families in accordance with preferred values and shared interests. Our beloved country is in a state of emergency!

People are looking for answers; they are looking for hope. America is too great and too remarkable to finish this way. The world desperately needs a strong and healthy United States, and as individual citizens, we deeply desire to pass the priceless treasure of freedom to our children and grandchildren. Despite all the concerns and high-stress anxiety that people are experiencing, there is a silver lining amid the storm clouds of distress. Each of the issues mentioned above can change for the better. In my understanding, there are two absolute essentials needed for the cure. First and foremost, although it is not the focus of this book, America is facing a spiritual problem. Having been founded on fundamental biblical principles, we have now come to the point of virtually criminalizing God within the public square and within the halls of government. The church, once a major voice for morality and justice, is bizarrely absent from being a trusted guide to help navigate through perilous times. Nonetheless, it is my deep conviction that the many issues we are facing can be remedied by means of a spiritual awakening and a return to the principles of character, decency, and a healthy fear of God. By so doing, I think we would discover that answers, indeed, do still exist. But the topic of addressing spiritual problems is a topic for another book. For now, there is another ray of hope, an opportunity that shines in the face of every American that should be recognized, heeded, and engaged. And although it may seem a difficult task to turn our national "ship" around, we still have the potential to do so by directly addressing and resolving problems using the tools we have at hand.

The challenges we face are not caused by fate or the Bard's "outrageous fortune." Every issue we face is the outcome of decisions, and these choices are being made by leaders. Just as decisions have consequences, leadership also has consequences. And it is from this perspective that our current national "emergency" has a degree of hope. Those leaders who have made poor decisions can and should be replaced with better stewards for America's future. Our system of governance allows the people to elect new public servants who can reverse or alter old decisions and correct the outcome of harmful consequences. But this can only happen once a gut-check of reality and action is interjected. I have already mentioned several serious problems facing America, but there is one additional threat that rises above all others: It is the *one* issue that singularly has the power to destroy America almost instantaneously. And the most frightful aspect of this threat is that *if* it takes a foothold, America cannot recover. The glories of our past will be forever lost to the powers of a cruel world, one void of individual freedoms and instead, overflowing with oppression by egocentric and power-hungry leaders. This is the greatest threat facing America:

Election Integrity

Voting is a civic Sacrament.
—REV. THEODORE HESBURGH, CSC

Ours is a nation that cherishes freedom. We are a collection of people comprising varying races, worldviews, and interests. As Americans, we unite under the eternal yearning for individual liberty. And as a safeguard for protecting that most sacred right, the people of this country have a voice in determining who their leaders will be. If we don't like the direction our current representatives are taking us, we can replace them. It happens every election. In fact, the ballot is the single most powerful tool Americans wield to hold their representatives accountable to policies that align with the majority, and policies that defend unalienable and constitutional rights that protect us all. If elected leaders fail to adequately represent their constituents, they should face the inevitable wrath of voters at the next election. They can and should be removed. It's a beautiful and effective system we possess!

By specific design, we are a nation whose political structure is based upon the will of the people, the voice of the majority, and the "consent of the governed." But what if our ability to replace inferior leaders is taken away? What if the voice of the people is denigrated and another person or group determines leaders for us? Just imagine, what if we had no voice at all? What if the constitutional right to be a self-determined society that chooses our own leaders, laws, and structure was strictly forbidden? What if our votes didn't even matter and elections were effectively rigged? Worse yet, what if I told you that dystopian reality may be closer than we think?

It's more than a dreadful scenario for conspiracy theorists, it's a terrifyingly realistic future. This book is not a prognosticator of doom; it is a klaxon of hope and defiance. Our great nation is not beyond hope. Our challenges may be more complicated than those endured by past generations, but they can be solved. The threat is real, and the time to act is now. The intent of this book is not political, but some will say otherwise.

So let's get a few things out of the way here and now:

- I am a Christian and served as a pastor for over 25 years prior to being elected to Congress.
- I am a conservative who holds to our Constitutional rule of law.
- I am a Republican.
- I recently lost a race for Secretary of State in Georgia.

None of those facts changes anything. This book is not intended to be a comparison between Republicans and Democrats. Rather, the intent of this book is a treatise on integrity. As a patriot and American, it is my duty to expose an enormous danger looming over the heads of my fellow countrymen. We must set aside political bias and canned talking points and have an honest discussion about a potentially nation-changing threat. There is an 800-pound gorilla inside our national "home," and it is angrily threatening our existence. We must deal with the monster. This book is, in its most basic message, simply about integrity, something we all should be passionately committed to protecting. But to do so, we must make every effort to look at the facts and try our best to separate ourselves from political posturing.

Elections are not ultimately about who wins or loses. Elections are about the voice of the people being heard, period. The overwhelming majority of people can accept the outcome of an election (though they might be deeply disappointed if their candidate loses), but no one should be willing to accept an unfair voting system. Losing a hard-fought election is one thing, but losing by deceit and duplicity is unacceptable and cannot be tolerated.

To be sure, no free society can ultimately survive unless it is rooted in a foundation of integrity, honesty, and virtue. And these axioms must be present within the public as well as the public servants. They must also exist within the various systems by which the country operates, and accountability is dynamism that enables a just society to prosper. But of all those traits and more, arguably the most important is integrity. Genuinely, what good are words or ballots if the system that operates them and tallies them has lost the people's faith? Personally, through my faith in Christ and through my family and life experiences, I continue to learn the importance of integrity. No doubt, I still have much to learn, but I have sincerely sought to carry that virtue to the pulpit, into politics, and throughout the rest of my life in public service. That is why I can't stay silent.

This book is not a reaction to one campaign or electoral season. I'm not writing to appease the ego or frustrations of any one person or party. I'm writing to reaffirm and restate for all the importance of these fundamental values upon which our nation is founded. And more specifically, if we don't address the pernicious influences that undermine them, by the time we realize the damage they've done, it will be too late. Democracy is so powerful yet so frail. It can overcome evil empires, but if we are not vigilant in protecting it, it can easily slip through our hands without us even realizing it.

Within the following pages, we will press to defend the voice of the people. In fact, to do so is the "magic wand" that we all possess. When our elections are safe, secure, and utilized, no country in the world can compare with our potential and strength; but allow the process of our elections to be weakened, compromised, or removed, and our future is as bleak as the fallen Roman Empire, which was once considered the only permanent global force in the world. The topic at hand could be the single most important issue facing Americans. Elections are the primary tool we have to let our voices be heard and to determine our nation's political leadership and future. So take up your "wand," grip it with all your might, and don't let go. Your nation is depending on you to properly use it and pass it to future generations. Friends, America cannot lose this battle for integrity!

1

Cutting My Political Teeth

Better is a poor man who walks in his integrity than a rich man who is crooked in his ways.

—PROVERBS 28:6

Our lives begin to end the day we become silent about things that matter.

—DR. MARTIN LUTHER KING, JR.

I T SHOULD HAVE BEEN one of the happiest and most rewarding days of my life. Instead, it was one of the worst, one that still fills me with disgust and remorse. Make no mistake, being a U.S. House of Representatives member is an incredible honor and something I will forever cherish. Words can't express the solemn joy of serving in that capacity for four terms, and I am humbled deeply by the privilege to have represented the 10th Congressional District in Georgia. But my first day as a newly elected member of Congress could not have been more enlightening and troublesome. It amplified the reasons why I so deeply abhor Washington, D.C., and why integrity matters.

———————

I'm a relatively simple man. I come from an ordinary and, frankly, some would say a nonimpressive background. My parents were both from Georgia; Mom grew up as a tenant farmer in middle of the state, raising cotton and other crops. Her family was tightly knit and worked hard to make a living. My father grew up in the north Georgia mountains in an era where everyone in that region of the state was poor and seemed to be in a constant state of survival from one month to the next. Upon graduating from high school, both of my parents moved to Atlanta in search of a better life. After meeting one another at a boarding house, they fell in love and soon were married. Both possessed a strong work ethic and held a deep commitment to loving God and family.

After trying his hand at several different jobs, my dad finally started a concrete construction company that became the primary means for our family throughout my childhood. Some years were thin, while others were flush, but my father always provided sufficiently. My brother and I had a wonderful childhood under the instruction and in the loving environment of two faithful and committed parents. We were raised in the church and never questioned the importance of faith. This instilled within us a clear understanding of right from wrong, respect for authority, and hard work. We were also taught to stand up for ourselves. As a young boy of about 10 years old, I recall a time when a bully was taking advantage of me at school.

I was gripped with fear and intimidation by his actions, but Dad instructed me very clearly and intentionally. He insisted that I take a stand and put a stop to the harassment. I clearly remember his words, "Never, never start a fight, son," he said, "but if you ever get into one, don't back away—finish it!" That advice seemed to take up residence deep within my being. The next time I was bullied at school by a boy nearly twice my size, I suppressed my fear and responded by hitting him as hard as I possibly could. My father's advice worked. He never bullied me again. No doubt, those words of Dad benefited me several times growing up, but little did I know how important they would become in the years ahead.

As for education, I was always an average student. It was not until my later years that I began to excel academically. But I was keenly motivated by wanting to do something that would make a difference in people's lives. At the age of 13, I had a personal encounter with Christ, and from that time forward became laser-focused on going into the ministry. Mom and Dad were very supportive of my sense of calling. Our family was very close, and we looked out for one another. Even today, although Mom and Dad have passed away, my brother, Thomas, and I meet every week for breakfast and remain the best of friends.

I met the girl of my dreams, Dee Dee, at Asbury University in Wilmore, Kentucky. Meeting her was like stepping into another world. Her family was off-the-chart so far as "amazing" is concerned. They have a heritage steeped in international influence. Among an enormous list of impressive accomplishments, her dad served in the U.S. State Department and spoke approximately eight different languages. Her mom, who also spoke several languages, came from Spanish royalty, including being in the family line of Argentina's first president, Bernadino Rivadavia. The stories and significant influence of her family in both U.S. history and global influence were something I had only read about. Her parents had lived in multiple countries, representing the United States, and had personal experience with world leaders. Dee Dee was born in England, then moved to Switzerland and Mexico before coming to her true homeland of America. Upon graduating from college, we got married and immediately moved to Texas for seminary training and education. Only God could have brought the two of us together, and He did!

Within a few years, our first daughter, Anna, was born, and our little family became our greatest delight. Life was moving fast, with me working three jobs while finishing my academic degrees. One of those jobs included my first pastorate at Sycamore Baptist Church in Decatur, Texas. It was a fantastic place to begin our ministry experience. The church people loved us deeply, and together, we all enjoyed being part of a growing and vibrant church. So many down-to-earth necessities for effective ministry were fashioned in us during those days. We absolutely loved our time at Sycamore. In fact, in every place we have lived since that time, we have planted a sycamore tree in honor of the incredible experience of our first pastorate.

Dee Dee made sure our home was a pleasant refuge, and together we decided it was best for her to be a stay-at-home mom so that she could raise and educate our children. After graduating from Southwestern Baptist Theological Seminary with a Master of Divinity degree, and later a Doctor of Ministry degree from Luther Rice Seminary, I accepted the pastorate at

First Baptist Church in Butler, Georgia. While there, our second daughter, Sara, was born, and our dream life with family and ministry was being realized.

People often ask me, "How does a pastor transition into becoming a politician?" Jokingly, I like to respond, "Well, you have obviously not been part of a Baptist church!" The similarities between the two, particularly as it relates to public speaking and dealing with people, are striking. Beyond that, members of Congress are only elected every two years, but as a pastor, it felt like I was up for "re-election" *every week!* Trust me, most pastors are well acquainted with political workings. Although I have never quite discerned the motivation behind the question, I have determined that it generally comes from an inquisitive mind. Some find it fascinating that a pastor would "fall" to the depths and depravity of Congress. Others are joyously captivated by the fact that a spiritual leader would take such a leap and try to expand Christian influence on a national stage. Either way, there is no doubt that being a pastor was prime training ground for me. Dealing with and leading people, often through extremely challenging times, has taught me the hard lessons learned only through experience. Developing staff, working with volunteers, casting vision and persuading people to embrace it, facing opposition and pushing through those conflicts without damaging the whole, all while growing the church and facing the challenges that come with growth, including new staff, more buildings, and so on, were indescribable preparation for Congress.

A pastor's primary role is to lead and equip his flock in the Word and the ways of God. To that end, I did my utmost to keep politics out of the pulpit, but I never backed away from a biblical message addressing current issues, even though some people might have viewed those as "political" sermons. But as a Bible-believing pastor, if Scripture speaks to an issue, it's not only "fair game" to talk about, but is in fact my responsibility to equip the congregants on how to interpret and respond to current issues through the lens of God's Word. Perhaps it was for this perspective that, although political involvement was never on my radar, it unfolded as a pathway that could not be swept aside. In my case, I did not go in search of politics, but politics went in search of me.

The United States of America is not a theocracy, but it is a nation whose principles and philosophy are rooted in the Judeo-Christian tradition. America's founding seems to clearly reveal that biblical principles are intended to inform, without dictating, the laws of this land. Leftists balk when you bring up such assertions. They maintain that secular morality is superior and that any Christian influence on laws should be barred under the principles of separating church and state. I'm not arguing for a biblical state, but a nation must have a set of morals. It must have shared ideas and a common ideology of freedom, liberty, and individualism. Without that foundation of integrity and unified moral underpinning, the American system of government, impressive though it may be, is ultimately no more than a city built on sand. I didn't seek out politics, but a political battle came after my flock, and it was my Christian duty to defend them.

Battling the ACLU

Beyond the obvious lessons learned by being a pastor, without any sense of anticipation as to what the future would produce, I was confronted with, and became involved in, a couple of significant legal challenges. Both propelled me to national attention. These two fights pushed me out of the "pulpit" and into an arena I had never imagined myself to be engaged in. They became the catalyst that eventually led me—kicking and screaming, I might add—through a door to Congress. The first battle brought me head-to-head with the American Civil Liberties Union (ACLU).

Following a few moves to different churches, I eventually became pastor of the First Baptist Church in Bethlehem, Georgia, located in rural Barrow County. The church started to grow rapidly and, in fact, became one of the fastest-growing congregations in the state, a position we held for several consecutive years. Amid the growth, we attracted a wide range of people, including several involved in local politics, including the county commissioners. Upon discussion and approval by the congregation, our church decided to purchase a large copy of the Ten Commandments and donate it to the county for display in the courthouse. In accordance with county commission policy, they held public meetings and debates about the gift, and following all the procedural requirements, they voted to approve the display. One of the commissioners, church member Bill Brown, literally took his own hammer and nails and placed the Ten Commandments in the hallway of Barrow County's courthouse. Indeed, the county commissioners, as well as our church family and the citizens of Barrow County by and large, were proud to exercise our First Amendment right to display the Ten Commandments and to acknowledge the Judeo-Christian foundation on which the values of our county rest. It was an amazing proclamation.

Everything was fine until one day in June 2003. I received a phone call from Bill asking if I had heard the news. "No," I replied, "what news?" With deep concern in his voice, he informed me that the ACLU had filed a lawsuit against Barrow County to remove the Ten Commandments from the courthouse as a matter of "separation of church and state." He said it would cost a fortune to defend the case and that the county did not have the financial ability to protect itself. I tried to provide encouragement to him and vividly recall at the time being unshaken and unconcerned with the ACLU's threat. I was confident that Barrow County had the right to display the Ten Commandments. I would soon discover that Bill had every reason to be concerned. He saw what was coming. The legal and political storm that awaited me would forever change the trajectory of my life.

The local newspaper and radio station immediately made the lawsuit against Barrow County the "talk of the town." The entire county seemed to rise in defiance of this injustice, and within days they were in unified resistance against the ACLU. By virtue of my position within the church, I became the recognized leader of the countywide movement. I never considered another option. Defending the Ten Commandments and our church members, some of whom were directly involved with the lawsuit, was the right thing to do. Firstly, my primary concern was protecting the congregation, yet I was not blind to the greater principles at stake. The First Amendment guaranteed our right to display the Ten Commandments, and we would not be told otherwise. No matter the legal fees or lawyer tricks of the ACLU, we would defend our rights. It appears the ACLU lawsuit marched down the aisle of our church, and for the most part, I welcomed the battle. Following an initial blast by local media, the Atlanta news was next to pick up the story. Within a week or so, national media began to swarm the little town of Winder, Georgia, and my phone began to ring off the hook requesting comments and interviews. In my mind, the hype would be short-lived and would soon pass like a summer thunderstorm. Surely everyone would recognize that removing the courthouse display would violate constitutionally protected religious liberty? Surely no one could deny the facts; the First Amendment clearly protects the display. Further, the decision to exhibit the Ten Commandments was made by elected officials, with the consent of their citizens. This is the way the government is supposed to work . . . right?

Regardless, the next step to be taken was convincing our county commissioners to take up the fight against the ACLU. I requested an opportunity to speak at their next meeting, and when the meeting occurred, it seemed the entire populace of Barrow County showed up. The room was packed, so much so that untold numbers had to stand outside, being unable to press themselves inside the large meeting room. I was confident that likely a few in attendance supported the ACLU, but without a doubt, the vast majority were present to urge their elected representatives to take a stand against the lawsuit. As the meeting got underway, I recall one of the commissioners commenting that an incredible number of people had shown up in support of the Ten Commandments. Then he said, "I'm curious if anyone here can quote the Commandments?" The place was hushed. It so happened that I had recently reviewed them, and as no one else stood up to accept the challenge, I slowly stood to my feet and began reciting the Ten Commandments. I made it through all ten, whew! A sense of relief seemed to fall upon the crowd, as did an even more profound sense of resolve to hold the commissioners accountable.

When given the opportunity to address the officials, I told them quite clearly that if they would take a bold stand and fight the ACLU, I would raise the money for the lawsuit. I would do everything in my power to make sure our legal defense did not cost the taxpayers of Barrow County. But the deal was firm: they would have to fight and not cave. After a brief discussion, they unanimously agreed to my offer. The crowd cheered with great enthusiasm, and I joined the celebration. The voice of the people had been heard and heeded by our commissioners. What a night! Although it was a great victory for the county, I had no idea that my life was about to change. I had no clue what I had just stepped into.

The county hired Herb Titus, an experienced attorney from Virginia, to defend the case. Under the advice of another individual, Charlie Wysong from Chattanooga, who had been through similar battles of his own and had now come to offer help for our efforts, we decided to have a countywide rally. It was one of several that would follow, but being the first, the rally could not have been better. Guest speakers included Alan Keyes, Alabama Chief Justice Roy Moore, Tony Perkins from the Family Research Council, Rick Scarborough with Vision America, Barrow County Commission Chairman Eddie Elder, and me. The media was present en mass, as was the crowd.

The battle was officially underway, and as a community, we were off and running, and the fundraising efforts were in full force. A local radio station, WIMO, asked me to provide weekly updates about the case. Within a relatively short time, those updates turned into a daily radio show, and over the course of time it eventually grew to the point that I was being heard on over 400 stations nationally every weekday. Speaking invitations began coming in by droves from across Georgia, even to Washington D.C., and a host of other places. The movement was drawing national attention. Many churches became actively involved, and because of the mantle being carried, I was elected first vice president of the Georgia Baptist Convention.

So many events took place over the next few years that I simply do not have time to share, but one fun story is worth passing along. Although it seemed each day consisted of another attempt to force me outside of my pastoral "comfort zone," I will never forget the horror and fear that shrouded me upon receiving a deposition notice from the ACLU. Being the leader of a movement that was openly opposing them, I knew they would love to do everything within their ability to discredit, or even destroy, my character. To describe my emotions as "trembling" is a significant understatement—"petrified" was a much more accurate depiction! I will never forget the day. Everything about the event seemed intentionally designed to create a sense of intimidation. For example, I had to wait outside the deposition room for what seemed like hours. A set of double doors separated me from the ones who, in my opinion, were on a mission to obliterate my existence. After what seemed to be the slowest day of my life, the time for my deposition came. I was ushered toward the double doors. When they were opened, there he sat, staring at me intently, the ACLU attorney. He was everything I had imagined. His hair was disheveled, a stain of coffee or other substance was on his shirt, and his tie was loosened and crooked.

As I entered the room, he tilted his head slightly and started wagging it back and forth. "Well," he said with all the disdain he could muster. "So, you're the Right Reverend Dr. Jody Hice?" Before I could even process the condescension of his statement, something deep inside me had already manifested an almost uncontrollable reply. I replied, "Yes, sir, I am Jody. But before we begin, would you mind if we started with a word of prayer?" "Um, well, uhh . . . well, sure, go ahead," he said. I honestly have no recollection of the prayer, but I remember praying for everything I could think of! After that, the aura of intimidation seemed to disappear. The lawyer was shaken. The deposition was a cakewalk.

The legal battle lasted approximately three years and cost about $300,000. I kept my promise, and the Barrow County taxpayers didn't have to pay for the lawsuit. In the end, we lost the case, and the Ten Commandments were ordered out of the courthouse. Seeing the Word of God expelled from the house from whose laws it was derived was a sad and dark day. How could this be? The Ten Commandments are present in multiple places in our nation's capital. They are the foundation from which our laws emerge. Heck, every dollar America mints clearly states, "In God We Trust."

Nonetheless, the Decalogue was removed from the courthouse, and we had to determine our next move. With the help of State Senator Ralph Hudgens and others, we directed our focus on the Georgia General Assembly. Then on May 7, 2012, after six years of dedicated involvement that resulted in an equal share of reassuring and disappointing days, our toils finally bore fruit. I was invited by Governor Nathan Deal to join him and others in a signing ceremony of a new law (HB766) that declared a nine-document historical exhibit, which includes the Ten Commandments, as legal to display in any government building in the state of Georgia. The General Assembly also, in a show of legislative resolve, placed the "Foundations of American Law and Government Display" in the state capitol, where it remains to this day. The genius of the bill was that it extended far beyond our little county. The bill served as a "stake in the ground" for other counties to follow.

Further, the new law declared that if a similar lawsuit to that in Barrow County were to arise anywhere else in Georgia, the state would fight the legal battle, not the individual county or municipality. Almost immediately, the display went up in Barrow County. Further, similar displays were unveiled in government buildings across the entire state. In all, it was nearly nine years of struggle, but victory at last! As life-changing as the Ten Commandments fight had been, it was only my first. Despite the widespread success, when the dust settled, I had every intent of putting politics behind me and returning to my primary focus, the church. Yet, even as I prepared to hang up my spurs, God laid out another battle for me. One that would eventually lead me to Congress.

Battling the IRS

During the previous conflict, I was traveling and speaking to multiple churches and groups. Along the way, I learned that many pastors feared getting involved with the Ten Commandments issue. Why? I anticipated all pastors would readily engage a battle for the Ten Commandments. Over time, it became clear that the reason was a legal provision called the "Johnson Amendment," which I was previously unaware of. It is true that while I was a pastor I used to receive threatening letters every election cycle from organizations like the Freedom from Religion Foundation (FFRF) and Americans United for Separation of Church and State warning me that the church and I could be sued and potentially lose our tax-exempt status if I were to address certain "political" issues from the pulpit. As a standard rule, I discarded such letters and continued with my regular routine. But as for the specific regulation that made so many pastors apprehensive about speaking on certain topics, I was not privy. Although I do not recall who contacted me, I received a phone call one day and was asked if I would consider challenging the IRS and their Johnson Amendment. Upon hearing the details of what the "amendment" was and realizing its impact on church leaders, I was all in: "*Yes*, count me in on the challenge!" The Johnson Amendment needed to be repealed.

Stated briefly, in 1948, Lyndon B. Johnson narrowly won an election for U.S. Senate. The reason for his narrow victory was due, at least in part, to a group of nonprofit organizations who believed him to be soft on communism, and they were effective in communicating that message to the voters of Texas. As a result, once he arrived in Washington, D.C., as a freshman Senator, he was on a mission to prevent such a thing from happening to him again. In July of 1954, without any debate on the Senate floor and by deciding behind closed doors, he managed to have a brief section inserted into the tax code, prohibiting all 501(c)(3) organizations from political involvement, including supporting or opposing a candidate. It came to be known as the Johnson Amendment. Although it is commonly believed that he never intended to attack churches and other houses of faith, most of them are organized under the nonprofit category as a 501(c)(3). Thus by default, all nonprofits, including churches, were restricted by the tax code from political engagement. For several decades following Johnson's maneuver, no church lost its tax exemption.

The amendment was never a serious issue until the early 2000s. Certain organizations began to see the law as a means by which to target and silence Christian voters. Initially, their main weapon was to send threatening letters like the ones I had received. Over time, having received such a letter every election cycle, church leaders became convinced that it was illegal for them to address certain issues from the pulpit. They censored themselves out of the debate, even on matters clearly taught in Scripture. If the topic could be considered "political," they refused to discuss it, being persuaded that doing so was a violation of the law. The Left's war of dishonest intimidation and fear was already infecting pastors and priests across the nation.

I had seen firsthand the negative impact this was having. Time and again, I had spoken with pastors who feared that taking a stand on something as basic and biblical as the Ten Commandments could lead to lawsuits and financial ruin. How could this be? If they wouldn't stand for the Ten Commandments, they would certainly not stand for other issues facing our nation, no matter how scripturally based. Churches were becoming unwilling to address anything deemed political, and as a result, a biblical worldview virtually ceased to be taught, and Christian involvement in politics was viewed as taboo. I am convinced that this is a primary reason why even today, churches are largely silent on so many issues. It is tragic! Although not enumerated in the Constitution, the "separation of church and state" mantra became largely understood as the law of the land and within churches across America. So when asked on the phone if I would consider challenging the IRS's Johnson Amendment, I was eager to do so.

Having already been through a "national" battle about religious liberty, it was not surprising that I also became a leader in this effort. After all, I was a pastor who had witnessed the tax code's negative outcomes and had personally been a victim of these threatening letters. With experience on my side, this effort to confront the IRS was unquestionably well-planned and organized. The Alliance Defending Freedom (ADF) had been watching the adverse impacts of the Johnson Amendment for years and decided to act. Being a large and influential group of brilliant attorneys, they developed a novel strategy. The basic premise was simple: If the IRS code were not resisted and ultimately defeated in court, the "bully stick" of intimidation and threats would continue to be used against churches to silence them. When considering the Constitution, most Americans understand that the First Amendment acknowledges religious protection to everyone, not just churches. But it is also true that the centerpiece of religious freedom is seen in the church, and the epicenter of the church's freedom is the pulpit. Constitutionally, the government cannot interfere with these sacred platforms, nor can they dictate what can and cannot be said. The purpose was clear: We must stand for the First Amendment and liberate church leaders to speak freely, without fear of punishment or harassment from the U.S. government.

As the plan materialized in 2008, 32 other pastors and I across American signed onto a challenge against the IRS. The nonprofit Alliance Defending Freedom was the legal team defending us and, hopefully, the ones who would liberate churches by dismantling the Johnson Amendment. We realized that to have an effective challenge meant that we must violate the tax code to such an extent that the IRS would threaten, revoke, or otherwise penalize our tax-exempt status. That being the case, we had to defy the tax code openly. The strategy was simple and straightforward but had never been done before. As pastors, we were plowing new soil to defend religious liberty.

On September 28, 2008, I along with 32 other pastors across America, challenged the IRS tax code and participated in "Pulpit Freedom Sunday." Our church, Bethlehem First Baptist, had already had many discussions before taking the stand, and they agreed that the battle was worth the risk. I will forever be grateful for the boldness they exhibited. Not surprisingly, the church was jam-packed that Sunday, with every media presence imaginable. All the major networks were in attendance, along with cable news, printed press, and the like. Even Nancy Pelosi's daughter was present; she was doing a documentary for HBO.

My message that Sunday provided a biblical perspective of two major issues: life and marriage. Then using the websites of the two presidential candidates, John McCain and Barack Obama, I showed how their positions on the subject either aligned with or contradicted a biblical perspective. Based upon the candidates' publicly stated beliefs in relation to scriptural teachings on the issues of life and marriage, I then urged our church family to vote for John McCain and admonished them not to vote for Barack Obama. Doing so was an obvious violation of the Johnson Amendment and the IRS code. Clicks and flashes were heard and felt throughout the entire auditorium. The seriousness of defiantly disregarding the IRS created a hushed sense of contemplation amid the legal and potential historical significance of the moment.

The next day, I sent a video copy of the sermon to the IRS, along with a letter. The letter essentially told the IRS that I had nothing to hide and therefore was sending a copy of the sermon for their review. I stated that, in my opinion, I had not violated the law nor the Constitution, but believed their IRS code (the Johnson Amendment) was unconstitutional, and I challenged them to come after me. The other 32 pastors took similar actions across America, and we waited for a response. Although one of the pastors received a slight reprimand, in the final analysis, the IRS did nothing.

So we gathered again as a group and decided to try it again. This second attempt drew more than a hundred participating churches from across the country, but still no response from the IRS. Pulpit Freedom Sunday soon became an annual event involving thousands of churches over the years, but when all was said and done, the IRS did nothing. I am convinced that they are fully aware that their attempt to dictate what can and cannot be expressed in churches is, without question, unconstitutional. Their continued silence allows the "threat" of losing tax-exempt status to remain and thus facilitates pastors to continue censoring themselves out of fear of "potential" legal problems. On a side note, as a member of Congress and with this being one of the primary issues that drove me to D.C., I was involved in getting a repeal of the Johnson Amendment passed in the U.S. House of Representatives on two different occasions, but both times the measure failed in the Senate. Indeed, I leave Congress with this being one of my greatest disappointments. Religious liberty must be defended and protected.

Once this battle began to subside, I once again thought I would be stepping back from politics and returning to my flock and fields. But the effort had garnered me significant notoriety. In addition to my congregation, I was now reaching thousands of Americans via my radio show. If there was a larger platform in my future, I thought it would be on the airwaves. Little did I know that God's true intent would see me entering the halls of Congress faster than I ever could have imagined.

2

That Horrible First Day in Congress

Lying lips are an abomination to the Lord, but those who act faithfully are His delight.

—PROVERBS 12:22

A politician thinks of the next election; a statesman, of the next generation.

—JAMES FREEMAN CLARKE

A S MENTIONED PREVIOUSLY, IT was never my intention nor was it ever on my radar to run for Congress. But the twin battles against government overreach pushed me into the national arena. My new radio program had at this point grown to be heard on more than 400 stations each weekday. A pathway was prepared that I never saw coming. In my mind, the future would involve having a broader voice through the radio broadcast, not holding public office. With that expectation, I resigned from the church believing God was leading me to engage the

Christian community to be "salt and light," in an America whose light was growing dim.

Leaving our congregation was one of the hardest decisions of our lives. The church was my second home, and the congregation our second family. They had nourished and supported us so much, as we had nourished and supported their relationships with God. I did not leave to chase the vanity of radio celebrity or to see my name in the newspaper. The fact is, I was never paid for my radio work. It was all done on spare time and at great personal sacrifice, both in monetary terms as well as time with the family. But as James 2:26 states, "For as the body without the spirit is dead, so faith without works is dead also." Dee Dee and I felt that God was leading us into a new chapter of influence, so we stepped out to follow His calling as we understood it. For us, it was a real large step of faith. We had no financial revenue stream by which to live, and we had no "Plan B." But we had a vision and a calling. Before I left the church, I promised myself that no matter how large my platform might become the words I preach and the life I live would remain the same. Proverbs 18:12 says, "Before destruction the heart of a man is haughty, but humility goes before honor." My mission was simple but difficult to practice: to stay humble before the Lord, to follow Him as best as I knew, and to not fear man or circumstances, but trust God to lead my steps.

Without going into laborious details as to how the run for Congress transpired, the short story is, three weeks after I resigned from the church, our representative at that time, John Linder, announced his retirement and that he would not seek re-election. Almost immediately, people started contacting us and asking me to consider running for Congress. For several weeks, it was a whirlwind of activity and soul-searching. But after much prayer and seeking counsel from trusted friends, my wife and I concluded that we should proceed. I would eventually run twice, the first time losing in 2010 to Rob Woodall (John Linder's chief of staff) in a runoff election, and then running again in 2014 and winning in yet another runoff, this time with Mike Collins. The second opportunity came as the result of district lines being redrawn. Although we did not move, our district changed from GA-7 to GA-10. Woodall was representing the 7th district, and Paul Broun represented the 10th. But Broun decided to run for U.S. Senate in 2014, so once again, an open seat was before us. As was the case four years previous, when Broun announced his bid for Senate, we were inundated with people asking us to consider running one more time. Like we had done in the first race, weeks of intense soul-searching, prayer and counsel became our daily diet, and eventually, Dee Dee and I again agreed, somewhat reluctantly so, that God was calling us to enter the arena once more.

I never could have imagined the demands of a federal campaign. In rather short order, our team was in place, and then we literally worked nonstop for nearly two years. The team, each of whom remain some of our most trusted and loyal friends to this day, were solidly committed to a well-planned, well-financed, well-executed strategy that would basically translate into virtually every moment of our lives being accounted for until election day. Dee Dee and I had no money to speak of, so a demanding fundraising commitment was required. Although it had to be done during the Ten Commandment battle, the fact is that I have a marked aversion to raising money! But it had to be done for the campaign, and because we believed God had called us to this, I resolved to do whatever was needed to run a competitive race. Mallory, the fundraiser, pushed me hard, but she also kept a positive attitude and attempted to make it fun (frankly, she never succeeded at that part). But no doubt, the whole effort would have been much more grueling without her tremendous people skills, particularly regarding the way she managed some-one like me, who dreaded every fundraising phone call. Jordan and Kaitlyn became the masterminds for the campaign itself. Their work ethic and knowledge of each detail that was needed for a winning campaign consisted of both political brilliance and masterful strategic thinking. It did not take long for me to realize that the assembled team was profoundly superb.

So I made the decision that if the race were going to be lost, it would not be because I failed to do something that was asked of me. I decided that whatever they requested, I would do it. Looking back, that was the right decision, but it was a brutal one. The demands and expectations were endless. But for every-one on the team, and for all who would join later, there was no doubt that the bar had been placed high, and we would not lose due to lack of work, planning, faith, or money. They made it an enjoyable and rewarding operation. The atmosphere was filled with high amounts of vision, excitement, character, ethics, and very hard work. We all became like a family. I will never forget the relief of Election Day finally arriving. Literally, there was nothing more that we could have done, as every ounce of energy had been placed on the table. No stone had been left unturned. So election night came with great anticipation. I will never for-get the throng of people, most of whom had joined the effort in various capacities. The election numbers started coming in that night, and our grassroots efforts, along with every aspect of the strategic plan had unfolded flawlessly. We dominated virtually the entire district. It was, indeed, a sweet victory.

Following a well-earned celebration with awesome friends, reality began to gradually sink in: I was headed to Congress! Having never been elected to any political office previously, the learning curve for Congress was huge for me. But one thing was certain: I had been very clear on the campaign trail regarding my convictions and was very outspoken regarding my core principles. That message had soundly resonated with the 10th Congressional District of Georgia that I was now entrusted to represent. Being a man of my word, I was eager to stand firm in Washington, D.C., even if it resulted in negative political consequences, which indeed would happen over the next eight years. It is one thing to be vocal on the campaign trail and outspoken on the radio; it is quite another matter entirely trying to express those convictions in a place as crooked and deceptive as D.C. I was a pastor. For the most part, I trusted people and took their words at face value. Conversely, when I give my word, I keep it. Little did I realize the "sausage mill" I was about to enter was more slimy and less dignified than I could have ever imagined. The delusional trickery by which the D.C. world operates would make the devil blush.

From a very practical perspective, I'm a firm believer in effective leadership and fully embrace the organizational reality that everything rises or falls on leadership. Every institution, including Congress, needs strong servant-leaders, not self-serving ones. In 2014, John Boehner was Speaker of the House, and I, along with millions of other Americans, believed him to be a poor leader, someone who personified the D.C. swamp. I had been quite vocal that if elected, I would vote against Boehner's bid to be Speaker of the House. That vote would be much more challenging than I had anticipated.

For newly elected members of Congress, the first official task before being sworn in is to attend orientation week, and then elect leadership for the upcoming Congress. The meeting to elect leadership for the 114th Republican Conference was held on Thursday afternoon, November 13, 2014. Obviously, Speaker Boehner and his team were keenly aware of my position regarding opposition of his leadership, and they tried to convince me to support him in the conference meeting. It was made clear to me that being a "team player" was the way to gain good committee assignments and to become an influential member of Congress, which they all knew I would be, so they said. As the conversation went back and forth for some time, I finally convinced them that I had made a promise to my district and would not change my vote. They reluctantly left me alone, so I thought.

As I entered the large assembly room in the Longworth House Office Building on that Thursday morning, I was taken aback by its beauty. The drapery, columns, and chandeliers were stunning. With a capacity of approximately 450 people, it was more than ample for the 241 Republican members and members-elect like me. A huge food buffet was waiting for us in the back of the room. It was BBQ with all the fixings, including an impressive choice of desserts. Something I would learn with time is that if the food at a conference meeting was unusually good, we were either in trouble for something, or the expectations and demands that were about to be presented by leadership would be hard-pressed upon us. I would also learn that if anyone didn't comply with the expectations, other consequences could be anticipated.

With unusually punctual timing, the meeting was called to order, and leadership elections were underway. By design, these elections are conducted by "voice vote" rather than secret ballot to embarrass and intimidate individuals who might dare speak against the coronation of the anticipated leaders. When their "soft diplomacy" of coercion fails, legislators have no qualms about using "hard diplomacy," including public shaming and other undesirable consequences. I would discover that truth soon enough. Nonetheless, not knowing anyone in the crowd, I sat near the back, which was a mistake from the perspective that to be heard for a voice vote, I would have to be loud in my objection. On the other hand, being staunchly committed to my opposition, I presumed being loud would be just fine. To be honest, you can do all the theoretical "imagining" possible before a moment like this, you can envision all the potential scenarios as to what it will be like, but until the time comes to be counted, there is no way to adequately describe the experience. Then it happened.

John Boehner was nominated to be re-elected as Speaker, and a voice vote was called, "all in favor of John Boehner being elected Speaker of the House, let it be known by saying, 'Aye.'" The affirmation was deafening and disturbingly one-sided. Then the chair continued, "all opposed to John Boehner being elected Speaker of the House, let it be known by saying, 'No.'" To this day, I still can hear my voice echoing off the large ceiling, "NO!" I cried, the only man entire room to do so. The people in front of me turned around to see what idiot had just uncovered his political nakedness with dramatic ignorance in front of the entire Republican Conference. Honestly, I heard no other voices of opposition, although a few colleagues later claimed to their local newspapers that they had voted against the Speaker. If true, they were very quiet in their disapproval of him. I will let that stand by itself. But I do know without any doubt that at least one person had been quite vocal, and I was proud to have done what I promised to do. But it seemed immediately like I was then looked upon by the entire conference as a troublemaker rather than a team player.

So there I sat, feeling very alone in my extremely public opposition to the leader of our conference and the person who would potentially be third in line to become president of the United States. But deep inside, I felt good. I had not come to Washington to merely float downstream like a dead fish. I had come to swim upstream. I was there to make a difference.

Following the election of our Republican leadership and the media hype that naturally accompanied it, efforts were immediately underway for "phase two" of Boehner's re-election plan. Candidly, at the time, I was not even aware that a second phase existed. I had been led to believe that the vote for Speaker was finalized in the conference meeting and my vote was a resounding "No." I could not have been more wrong, nor could I have been more blind to a trap that had been set. It was all a deception, and I stepped right into it. My experience in Washington, D.C., would soon expose depths of defilement that I could hardly imagine, and even then, it was but the tip of the iceberg that I would experience over the next eight years. Call me naïve. I am probably guilty of the claim. But until proven unworthy of trust, I generally believe people when they look me in the eye and confidently tell me something. I have since learned that inside the D.C. bubble, it is foolish to believe what you are told at face value. This is a world I was not accustomed to, and the initial learning experience would prove to be one of the most dreadful days of my life.

Here's the truth: Elections for Speaker of the House involve a two-step process—one takes place in the conference meeting, and the other is followed in January by a vote on the House Floor. Following my loud opposition in the conference meeting, Republican leadership unleashed the proverbial political "hounds" to correct the error of my ways. They told me that the "real" vote for Speaker was the one we had just completed in the conference meeting and that I had fulfilled my promise by voting "No" for Boehner. They commended me for doing what I had said I would do. But then the conversation turned. "You heard the conference vote overwhelmingly in favor of Boehner. You did your job by opposing him, but now is the time for unity. When we go to the House Floor, it's critical that we show a unified front to America. The vote on the floor is simply a formality. The 'real' vote took place in the Conference. Now is the time to recognize the will of the Party and unify behind it." John Boehner himself called to convince me of the same.

Their assertion sounded reasonable, and I fully understood the power and importance of unity. I had preached many sermons about unity. Regarding the matter at hand, I had made my lack of support for Boehner known, but my attempt to oppose him had undoubtedly failed. Had I been the *only* one to oppose him? It certainly appeared that way to me. But listening to these people talk, it somehow made sense to accept their claim; I had done my job by voting "No."

On the other hand, something about their words didn't feel right. At the time, I had no trusted friends in D.C. from whom I could seek advice. I vividly recall agonizing over this decision with my campaign consultant and newly chosen chief of staff, David Sours. Frankly, they seemed as bewildered by the dilemma as I. Nothing was accomplished by our discussions other than greater uncertainty. Nonetheless, upon mounting pressure and persuasive words, I finally agreed to join the unified "team" and support Boehner on the floor.

In what seemed like no time at all, the big vote arrived. It was January 6, 2015. On this day, I would be sworn in as a member of Congress. Family and friends had made the long journey from Georgia to Washington, D.C., to witness the historic day and celebrate the grand event. The swearing-in ceremony was, itself, somewhat of a letdown. It consisted of all 435 members sworn in simultaneously and was utterly devoid of pomp or personal sentiment. Afterward, we were given a photo-op with Speaker Boehner, with one hand on the Bible and the other lifted as though taking an oath of office. It felt phony, and indeed, it was. To be perfectly honest, when the events of that day were over, the last thing I wanted was a picture with the Speaker, and frankly, to this day, I have no idea where that picture is located. Hopefully, it landed in the trash, where it belongs.

Following the brief swearing-in of all members, we held our first vote on the House Floor, an election for Speaker of the House. Unlike the voice vote in the Conference meeting, this election was by roll call, and when your name was called, you stood up and declared your choice for Speaker. To my utter amazement, as the roll was being called, some of my Republican colleagues were voting for someone other than John Boehner. I was stunned! When the "real" vote occurred in the Conference meeting, where were these people? They told me the vote on the floor was a rubber-stamped vote of unity and one of agreement as a party. This was supposed to be a mere formality of the over-whelming affirmation Boehner had received on November 13. What was happening?

I had personally given Boehner my word that I would sup-port him on the floor. My nerves grew tense. I felt hot and began to sweat. My body felt weak, and I literally began to tremble. Before I knew it, I heard the clerk call my name, "Mr. Hice from Georgia?" In what seemed like the most difficult physical move I had ever made, I shakily rose to my feet and said, "John Boehner." Something inside me felt like it had just died. I sat down and was entirely numb, wanting to run off the House Floor and burst into tears. As it would end up, 24 Republicans voted against Boehner that day; it should have been 25, but I had given my word. Never would I have voted for John Boehner had I not been deceived into agreeing to do so. My agreeing to support him had come only after being told that my "No" vote was the "real" vote, and it had already taken place in the November Conference meet-ing. To the depths of my soul, I felt nauseous. I had been lied to and had taken the bait. That place is full of lies and deceit. But how could I explain this to the 10th District? It would be diffi-cult. Certainly, they would believe that I lied to them, because my "roll call" vote had been televised and publicly displayed in favor of Boehner despite me clearly stating on the campaign trail that I would not support him. They would never understand that I alone had strongly voiced opposition toward him in the Conference meeting. They would never believe my roll call was the result of being lied to regarding the need for party unity. I would be viewed as an untrustworthy representative.

Indeed, it was exceedingly awkward visiting with friends afterward. All I wanted was to get away and be with Dee Dee.

After what seemed to be forever, we finally said our "good-byes" to all those who had come, and each of them treated me with kindness and grace. But it was hard to face them; I felt compromised and dirty. Finally, Dee Dee and I were alone for the first time in our temporary apartment. We were both very quiet, stunned by the day's events. Then suddenly, as from a geyser involuntarily spewing forth steam, she burst into tears and in deep grievous tones bellowed out, "Why? Why did you vote for him?!" She was profoundly aware of the promises I had made during the campaign. She knew me to be a man of my word. She had no way to internally reconcile my actions. Nothing made sense. Her tears quickly turned to uncontrollable sobs, and she could no longer speak.

My wife, who was there to celebrate a great day, cried her heart out and felt as though I had lied to the 10th district by breaking my commitment on the very first public vote. I had nothing to say. I had been deceived and entrapped. I had let Dee Dee down; I had broken my promise to the 10th District. At that moment, I despised myself. I had no defense. In utter brokenness, I fell to the floor. On my very first day in Congress, I was already a failure, someone who had broken his word and had drunk the D.C. water. It was the most horrible experience. I had serious thoughts of resigning. I do not recall ever feeling so low and ashamed. I was not fond of D.C.

It took months to rebound from that day. Even now, years removed, the sense of disappointment still haunts me. Deep inside, after that experience, Dee Dee and I both developed a disdain for Washington. We had been stained by its filthy practices and would never feel the same about politics. The lessons learned that day were brutally honest. For several weeks, there was a small voice inside me; I believe it was the voice of God that gently reassured me, "This is the best thing that could have happened. Now you understand how Washington works. You've learned a lesson you will never forget, and it will make you a much wiser Congressman." Indeed, that voice has proven accurate. Within months, the House Freedom Caucus was organized, and I was honored to be one of the original members. That group, behind the courageous leadership of Mark Meadows's actions to file a motion to "vacate the chair," was effective in resisting the continued actions of John Boehner, and he was forced to resign.

Why do I share all this? We all know that government officials often have a loose affiliation with facts and truth. It is not a new revelation to anyone reading that politicians will often tell you one thing while doing another. Nor is it a shock to admit that deception comes with unsettlingly natural ease to many leaders on Capitol Hill. To be sure, everyone reading this has also been lied to, and many have experienced similar anguish. Perhaps you responded to your situation better than I did, and perhaps you were not nearly as naïve. But those abysmal encounters that result in deep remorse and an utter sense of failure are often life-changing. Each of us is defined by how we respond to them.

I share this personal experience, this embarrassing and humiliating failure because it became one of the most consequential moments in my entire legislative career. The lessons learned would inform every choice I made for the duration of my tenure. I arrived in D.C. feeling good about my ability to be strong, courageous, and consistent. I was there to "swim upstream" and to make a difference, but I had been blindsided by deliberate misinformation and outright lies. This is the way D.C. operates. As I looked back on that week, it was alarming to recognize how the dishonesty had not been subtle, it had worked its vile activities in plain sight. Indeed, this type of experience is the way many members of Congress succumb to The Swamp. A snare is set, uniquely designed for that member, and once the trap's intense grip closes, it forces many to yield and feel helpless against the destructive forces of the D.C. tactics. The initial "traps" are mostly designed to show members that they are powerless to stop the huge system. In fact, the power brokers want every member to be aware that D.C. can destroy them and their political careers if they don't comply. As a result, many in D.C. sell their souls and in exchange are given a false sense of security, protection, money, and "cover" from the evil culture that forces submission through intimidation and extortion. I had believed we were off to a good start until the "swamp trap" seized me. It was only then that reality sunk in. Fortunately, in my case, once reality enlightened my understanding, it was not too late to change. I learned from the experience and made adjustments that helped direct me for eight years in the Washington, D.C., mire.

Applying the Lesson

On a much larger scale and in a more critical way, a similar scheme of deception is currently underway in America. We are told that everything is fine and that our suspicions relating to elections and other concerns are petty, conspiratorially driven, and incorrect. In fact, the mantra goes so far as to say that you are a dangerous threat to democracy if you do not comply with the politically correct position. Not only is it becoming more objectionable to publicly vocalize our concerns, but it is also considered wrong to question what they claim as "real." And like me wanting to be a "team player," who wants to be considered dangerous? We naturally want to be on the team, and we certainly don't want to experience the consequences of being tagged and targeted as a danger to society. Again, most people recognize that the huge political machine that encompasses our government, like a prowling monster, can destroy our lives, our livelihood, and our reputation.

But the stakes are too high for us to retreat. Tough times call for tough people. If we do not stand to be counted at this hour, I do not have sufficient confidence that America, as we have known it, can long survive. The ability to pass freedom to the next generation depends on our willingness to step into the arena now. And if we don't do so at this historic moment, I am telling you, it will be too late. A movement is already underway to eliminate our capacity to self-govern. And the eradication of this one principle will destroy America. To what am I referring? Election integrity. Think I'm overstating the truth? Just listen to the accusations and denunciations directed toward those who have been outspoken on the issue.

These days, if you are one who thinks our electoral system might have structural flaws, you're accused of being an "election denier" and automatically dismissed as a dangerous threat to our system of governance. I know. I've experienced it. And just as the darkest day of my life turned into an indescribable learning experience that produced effective and wise change, we must also face the truth about elections. We can't assume everything is fine just because D.C. and the legacy media tell us so. If their communication is really accurate that elections in America are totally secure, then why are Democrats so focused on passing legislation that would permanently federalize them? If there are no problems, then there is no reason for such aggressive actions.

Difficult as it may be, try to imagine how an immense constitutional change of this magnitude could possibly transpire. Any deceptive scheme of this nature would include the accusation that all election naysayers were conspiracy theorists and dangerous, and thereby, an attempt would be made to lull ordinary people into inaction. The task of federalizing elections is much easier to accomplish if the opposition is quiet and unresponsive.

Make no mistake, we must swim upstream on this issue. I do not believe it is an exaggeration to say the biggest threat to democracy is the loss of fair elections. Don't be distracted by the radical noise asserting that those individuals who have questioned the potential lack of election veracity are the problem. And remember, no matter how great the hostility may grow or how ferocious the attacks become, authentic transparency is the only way to secure election integrity. That's the message of this book. The future of America rests upon the way we respond to this issue.

3

My First Visit to the Oval Office

So, whoever knows the right thing to do and fails to do it, for him it is sin.

—JAMES 4:17

The ultimate measure of a man is not where he stands in moments of comfort and convenience, but where he stands at times of challenge and controversy.

—DR. MARTIN LUTHER KING, JR.

M Y FIRST TWO YEARS in Congress were spent under the Obama administration. As such, it was no surprise that during his terms in office, I was never invited to visit the White House unless it involved a special event such as the annual Christmas Ball, which is certainly nice but rather artificial so far as official meetings are concerned. It wasn't until Trump was elected that I finally had an opportunity to visit the White House formally and officially.

When the invitation came, he had been president for only a couple of months, and I was excited beyond words. I will never forget the call from my senior aide, Tim Reitz, who would later become my chief of staff. "Sir," he said, "the president has requested a meeting with you in the White House tomorrow." To be perfectly honest, my first thought was, *Why does the president want to see me?* My mind immediately had a flashback of times when the high school principal requested a meeting. Those were not generally invitations that were received with positive anticipation. But upon further contemplation, I concluded that the president was being a thoughtful leader and was inviting different members of Congress for a "get acquainted" meeting.

After all, Republicans now controlled the levers of power in Washington, governing both the House, the Senate, and most important, the White House. The previous two years had us confined in the tail years of the Obama administration, which was a miserable time, politically speaking. To me, Trump's invitation represented big changes in D.C., changes for Republicans on the Hill and changes for America as a whole. The more I pondered it, the more persuaded I was about the motive behind his invitation. The president's request was beginning to form and make sense in my mind. But at the end of the day, whatever his reason, when the president of the United States extends an invitation to meet with him, all other appointments on the calendar take a back seat.

The next day, when I arrived at the White House security gate, special treatment was granted, which is standard practice for all members of Congress. Within minutes, I was inside the White House waiting to see President Trump. To my surprise, I was not the only one waiting. There were several other members who were there for the same meeting. Initially, that reality was a little puzzling, but I concluded that he wanted to get acquainted with as many members as possible and as quickly as possible, so small groups were the best solution. Again, that made sense to me. It still had not occurred to me that another motive was directing this gathering.

Within a short time, we were all escorted into the famous Cabinet Room, which boasts a beautiful long wooden table, leather chairs, and an overall presence that demands attention and respect. In all, there were about 18 of us present, probably most of whom were enjoying their first visit to the White House. Taking a deep breath, I thoughtfully tried to absorb the moment. It was surreal. There was an unmistakable sense of pride and anticipation in the historic room where so many critical meetings had occurred throughout America's history. I breathed it all in. Then while various conversations were underway among those in attendance, suddenly the door opened, and President Donald Trump entered the room. Immediately, we all stood to our feet and began to clap in honor of our president. Adorned with his large smile, he welcomed us to the White House, then walked around the room greeting each of us individually. Following the initial greeting, he sat down at the center of the table with members to his right and left, and I was seated diagonally across from him, almost face to face. He started with a casual conversation and soon revealed a side of himself that most people are unaware of. His humor and ability to connect with people were stunning. Within minutes the entire room was bursting with laughter as he successfully removed all potential anxieties anyone might have had as to the purpose of the gathering. At this point, I was convinced that my original feelings were correct; we were there to get acquainted. He was masterful at "breaking the ice" and making everyone feel comfortable. He was the ideal host.

Then he paused, and looking around the room with a pleasant expression as though an idea of perfect aptness had just popped into his mind he said, "How many of you have never been to the Oval Office?" Several hands immediately raised, including mine. "Would you like to go there?" Wow! This day could not have been more perfect. It was the realization of every dream that a member of Congress could imagine. I was in the White House with the president of the United States, laughing and having a wonderful experience. He then led us into the Oval Office.

The room seemed smaller than I had anticipated, but its lack of size did not downgrade the absolute wonder of this magnificent office. It was, indeed, breathtaking. The president's gorgeous desk rested on one end of the room and a stately fireplace on the other side. But something was not right. The enticement of being escorted into the Oval Office had not been a spur-of-the-moment decision. Something else was obviously happening behind the scenes. A nice chair had been placed in front of the fireplace, and 18 other chairs were placed in horseshoe shape, starting on one side of the president's chair and going around to the other. The couches and other furniture that were typically in front of the fireplace had been moved. Although we were now the majority party with control of both chambers of Congress and the White House, the truth is that nothing happens by accident in D.C. We were not there for fun; this meeting was intentional . . . but for what? At the end of the day, everything in that city has a political purpose attached. The joyful feelings experienced in the Cabinet Room had now departed. Thoughts of caution began to whisper in my mind, *Something is strange here, be careful.*

After showcasing some of the pictures on the walls and various interesting artifacts in the revered office, the president then asked us all to be seated. Again, he treated us to a few moments of humor and relaxed conversation, when suddenly, from the back of room came a loud voice from the GOP deputy whip, Patrick McHenry. "Mr. President," he said, "I think now would be a great time for you to go around the room and have each member tell you where they stand on the American Healthcare Act (AHCA)." Likely, the pale expression on my face was evident to everyone. Internally I said to myself, *So, this is why they invited me to the White House!*

The bill that McHenry referred to was the creation of our new Speaker of the House, Paul Ryan. It was a lame attempt to repeal and replace Obamacare. The fact is, it did neither, and I was adamantly opposed to it. Speaker Ryan had developed his plan for the Republican Party and had named it, "A Better Way." But truthfully, his plan was status quo at best and was nothing better than a slower pathway to achieve Democratic ideals. Nonetheless, Ryan had convinced Trump that it was a good bill and something worthy of pressuring Republican members to support.

Acknowledging McHenry's request, the president agreed to put each attendee on the hot seat and have us answer directly to the president himself. I do not remember who was seated where, but I vividly recall Trump looking to his left, and while making direct eye contact, he asked the member, "So where do you stand on the healthcare bill?"

"Oh, Mr. President," he said, "I'm totally on board with you. Yes, sir, you can count on my support." The president nodded his head in approved satisfaction and then looked to the next, "What about you?"

"Yes, sir, Mr. President, I support the bill. I'm with you."

"Good," Trump replied, "it's a good bill; thank you for your support." I was beginning to get very nervous. There were six people ahead of me, and the first two had unwaveringly given their backing for the pathetic legislation. Four more until the president would lean into me with all the pressure of his position and the grandeur of the Oval Office.

One by one, each of the four offered their absolute support for a bill that was horribly flawed. Then he looked at me. Had there been a way of escape, I would probably have bolted. But staring directly into my eyes and anticipating continued support, he asked for my reply to the question at hand. "Mr. President," I said, "I cannot support the bill as it is." He sat back in his chair as if in disbelief and then glared at me while reacting with unconcealed irritation and forcefulness. The ensuing minutes seemed like an eternity. I felt as though I was being flogged. He vocally lit into me with no degree of mercy. And then from behind me, another voice spoke. To this day I do not know if it was vocalized loudly for the entire room to hear or if it was simply spoken into my ear. But Patrick McHenry, who had initially suggested this public accounting, came up behind me and said in a condescending tone, "You cannot say 'No' to the president of the United States!" Perhaps some people would have melted from that contention, but for me, his comment made me instantly mad. I immediately thought, *No one has the right to tell me what I can or cannot say or think.* At that point, the president continued staring at me. Without saying another word, he silently waited as the pressure mounted—he was providing me another chance to correct my viewpoint. To the best of my ability, I looked him straight in the eye and said, "Mr. President, I cannot support the bill." Having already delivered a verbal lashing, he jerked his head in strong disapproval. Then he decided to pressure the next member, using the example made from me as the standard for the next member to expect.

Seated to my immediate left was Ted Yoho from Florida. Perhaps it was because of what he had just seen happened to me, or maybe he had simply been awaiting his chance to speak. Either way, like me, Ted was part of the Freedom Caucus and when asked to give his position, he decided to be exceedingly forceful with his answer. While hitting his fist on the armrest of his chair, he forcefully and loudly decried, "I'm a *no!*" I have no doubt that his voice could have been heard several rooms away. His sharp answer seemed to surprise the president and made him pull back with his body language. He had no words to reply. He simply looked at Ted for a few seconds, then nodded his head and said, "OK." Seated next to Ted was another Freedom Caucus member, Tom Garrett from Virginia. In a similar fashion, he gave a firm "no" answer. It was like the dam had broken. One by one, members began to refuse any support for the bill. By the time all 18 had spoken, it had become evident to the president that he was not going to have enough votes to pass the bill.

By no means am I trying to imply that the bill failed because of my objection to the president's pressure in that meeting. In fact, I am quite confident that others in the room would have said "No" with or without me doing so. However, it so happened that I was the first one to object, and I will forever be thankful to have been placed in that circumstance. It was a moment of personal growth, as courage and conviction had to rule the day, not political appeasement. Not only was that a significant moment in my life, but in many ways, it was also a turning point in Trump's presidency. It became increasingly obvious that he could not trust Speaker Ryan. On the other hand, he seemed to appreciate the fact that there were members from the Freedom Caucus who stood up for what they believed, even under pressure. As a result, President Trump became good friends with members of the Freedom Caucus. I recall several times when the Freedom Caucus members were meeting, the president would call Mark Meadows, our chairman at that time. Mark would say, "Mr. President, we are having a meeting right now, and I am going to put you on speakerphone with all the members of the Freedom Caucus." In those days, Trump used to call us the "Freedom Guys," and we developed a strong and trusted relationship with him over the next few years. Several times, he extended invitations for us to join him at the White House for private discussions on various pieces of legislation and other issues. A picture of one of those meetings hangs in my office as a continual reminder of how my first meeting with him, uncomfortable as it was, turned into a healthy and treasured relationship.

The mainstream media takes a perverse amount of glee in portraying President Trump as a deranged narcissist, as someone who surrounds himself with supplicants and "yes-men." To be sure, he's not a man who enjoys being told no and even less that he's wrong. He is headstrong and stubborn in his beliefs and for the causes that he champions. However, there is nothing he respects more than a man willing to disagree with him. That day,

I stood my ground and refused to capitulate; other presidents would have exiled me, but Trump respected me. He respected the fact that I stood my ground amid pressure because that's also the way he operates.

I often wonder to myself, were it not for my earlier experiences with former Speaker Boehner, would I have been so steadfast in my opposition? Would my knees have buckled and my confidence caved? The truth is, regardless of how I voted in the case of Boehner, he would have won the speakership. But had I backed down in the Oval Office and placed my support behind the AHCA, things might have turned out differently. We will never know. As I stated earlier, I was not the deciding voice that day, but my stance did lead the way for others, and in that regard, it was an important stand.

Throughout our lives, God and the devil will put our integrity to the test. It could be something as small as whether to steal a candy bar as a child, cheat on an exam at school, or something as serious as opposing poor health care legislation to the president of the United States as a congressman.

Far often, the first challenges of integrity we face are of little consequence. Stealing that candy bar or telling that white lie to your parents likely won't make much of a difference immediately. The reason it matters is that those little tests lay the foundation for the men and women we will one day become. Every test of integrity God lays before us is a gift. It's an opportunity to become greater than ourselves. I like to think that God allowed me to be tested on my first day in Congress, knowing that I would fail. He did so not to punish me but so that when it really mattered in the years that followed, I would stay true to my integrity and fight for what I knew to be right. I most certainly have not passed every test since that time, but that first congressional failure became a strong motivator to do everything in my power to not repeat, and thereby regret, poor decisions. There is a great sense of personal gratification that comes with standing firm amid struggles. But the ability to stand firm in hard times is never automatic. It requires personal integrity and learning to be unwavering in the mundane and small things of life. Proverbs 20:7 says, "The righteous person walks in his integrity; his children are blessed after him" (NKJV). This verse lays forth a principle that I was taught as a youngster. Over the progression of time and repetition, either for good or bad, thoughts lead to decisions, decisions lead to habits, habits lead to character, character leads to a legacy. This is the power of integrity, and this virtue would be tested, as well as greatly needed, in my new role as a congressman.

4

Experiences
in Congress

*So, I always take pains to have a clear conscience toward both
God and man.*

—ACTS 24:16

*Integrity is a life where your beliefs and intentions are aligned
with your words and actions.*

—STEPHEN LOVEGROVE

OVER THE YEARS, MANY people have asked me, "What's it
like being a congressman?" Although it was the greatest
honor of my life, I can assure you that any assumption that it
is all glitz and glamour is far from the reality of public service.
Many Americans imagine congressional life as an endless series
of fancy receptions, marble buildings, black-tie events, fame,
media interviews, dramatic speeches, and daily critical votes
that impact the future of our republic. I must confess, I'm grin-
ning while writing this and thinking to myself, *Yes, but . . . .*

Some of these romantic notions did come true from time to time, but my experience involved the other side of the coin as well. In fact, it will not surprise me if future anthropologists conclude that congressional life is an unnatural phenomenon. Nowhere else on planet Earth will you find so many people doing so much work for so little progress. I've lost count of how many days I came home exhausted from a long day's work, only to look back and realize very little actually got done. In my case, the supposed "glitz" was quickly controverted by political reality. Generally, my daily schedule in D.C. was broken into 15-minute increments, consisting of one meeting after another, which were only interrupted by media interviews, committee hearings, or a series of votes on the House Floor. Frequently, someone on my staff would "brief" me about the next meeting or interview literally while we were walking down the hallway for the forthcoming encounter.

On a regular basis, lunch consisted of Georgia-grown peanuts, chips, and a Coke, all of which were supplied to our office by Georgia businesses. And the schedule didn't improve much when I was in the district. Being mostly rural, GA-10 included about 25 counties. As you can imagine, every Rotary Club, Chamber of Commerce, business, local media, GOP group, and church gathering wanted my presence, along with a long list of constituents who lined up at the office door for an appointment. Don't get me wrong; I sincerely loved being in the district and serving the people. That was a highlight of the job and was both fun and extremely fulfilling. But it was also time-consuming and exhausting. Dee Dee and I didn't have a vacation for the first three and a half years of my time in Congress. In all honesty, it was a stressful time for our family, and I very much disliked being gone from home so much. And added to the time away from family was the responsibility of staying "on top" of every issue while controlling emotions and disappointments brought about by the horrible changes taking place in our country and feeling powerless to turn it around. Then there was the constant aggravation of ridicule and vileness expressed through social media and political opponents daily, along with frequent threats of physical harm that were directed toward me or my family. Unfortunately, our society has become too accustomed to these practices, and these days, enduring such behavior is simply recognized as being a part of the job.

Moreover, most people are surprised to learn that I slept in my office when in D.C. And believe it or not, I was not alone in that arrangement. Probably about a third of the U.S. representatives make a "home" out of their offices. In my case, the routine each night involved retrieving a foldout cot from the closet and preparing it with sheets and pillows. The cleaning crew came each morning at 5:00 a.m., so my alarm awakened me at 4:45 a.m., when I would quickly arise and put the cot back in the closet and the sheets in their respective drawer. While the office was being cleaned, I went to the gym for a shower, and upon my return, there was ample time to prepare a cup of coffee, read the Bible for personal devotion, pray, and prepare myself for the upcoming meetings and events of the day.

Before mentioning a few of my experiences as a congressman, I must acknowledge the importance of having a quality staff. A member of Congress simply cannot survive without a great staff, they do so much! Our staff was known abroad for being super responsive and extremely professional. It seems there was nothing they could not handle. Without a question, they made me look a lot better than I am. Both in D.C. and in the district, they were unequivocally among the best in the nation, and we were a very close team, practically like family. And despite working very hard day after day and grappling through countless battles, and despite daily criticism from the Left, we really enjoyed being together. Probably the saddest part of leaving Congress was dismantling the team. Dee Dee and I love them so much.

One fun fact about the Hice office is that we allowed pets. In fact, we had four of them, three dogs and a rabbit. All the dogs came to us as puppies and literally grew to become effective "support" staff. Rocco, a bulldog, belonged to my chief of staff. His presence was so fitting for a member who represented the University of Georgia. Go Dawgs! Then there was Freya, arguably the most adorable English cocker spaniel you've ever seen. She belonged to Nathan Barker, my legislative director. Next was Lilly, a miniature golden doodle owned by Sarah Selip, my communications director. And finally, we had a Lionhead rabbit named Dublin. He belonged to Emma Settle, my assistant communications director. People came from all over Capitol Hill to visit our "office staff," and one member of Congress wrote a letter to Freya, which was probably the first time a pet ever received a letter from a sitting member of Congress. We tried to place our pets on a rotational schedule to not look so much like a zoo, but that didn't always work. Lilly was often too cute to be contained to just one day. Nonetheless, from the "humanoid" personnel to the pets, our office always produced smiles and good experiences for everyone who visited.

My senior staffers, Sarah, Nathan, and Tim, were not only consummate professionals but dear friends whom I remain in close contact with to this day. Tim's steady hand and strong leadership ensured we had one of the most effective offices on

Capitol Hill. His good nature and sense of humor helped make our office the tight-knit community I look back on with fondness and warmth. Nathan's deep legislative knowledge was an invaluable asset, especially with Nancy Pelosi springing massive spending bills on Congress in the 11th hour. His analysis saved me many sleepless nights that would have otherwise been spent pouring over bloated spending bills. Sarah was one of the youngest communications directors ever hired on Capitol Hill, for good reason. Her tactful messaging and clear insights into the 24-hour news cycle propelled me from a humble conservative congressman to a national political figure. It was a privilege and honor to lead such a talented team.

Although there are many sacrifices and hardships that come with being a member of Congress, there are also many indescribable and wonderful experiences and benefits, not the least of which was serving with some of the most incredible people in the world. I gained many friends and cherished relationships, most of which were built upon deep and mutual respect.

Without a doubt, my closest professional friendships consisted of, in my opinion, the cream of the crop in Congress. They are fearless warriors; they are members of the House Freedom Caucus (HFC). To me, they were the best of the best. They were not in D.C. for the purpose of seeking re-election or power. They were genuinely standing in the gap for millions of Americans who felt as though they no longer had a voice in Washington. I truly miss being in the trenches with them.

But beyond the friendships were some of the experiences that cannot be duplicated by any other job. For example, having the ability to travel to various countries as a representative of the United States is an awesome responsibility and honor, as is being part of a congressional delegation, whose purpose is to learn more about important matters related to our national interests. And oftentimes, those trips incorporated experiences that were overwhelmingly amazing, like landing on the U.S.S. *Ronald Reagan* aircraft carrier off the shores of Japan in the Pacific Ocean. And then, of course, being catapulted off the ship. Wow, talk about an adrenaline rush! Or being in Israel when the American Embassy was moved to Jerusalem from its former location in Tel Aviv. That was, to me, an experience of a lifetime.

There were so many different and magnificent experiences. For instance, I will never forget the unbelievable times of traveling on Air Force One with the president. The only appropriate description of such an experience is, spectacular! Vice President Mike Pence gave me the rare fortune of sitting in the cockpit of Air Force Two as we took off from Andrews Air Force Base in Maryland. Being someone who loves aviation, that was a surreal flight. Speaking of Air Force One, perhaps the most nonsensical thing I ever did was the time I refused an opportunity to fly with the president on Air Force One. Trust me, such a numbskulled choice is not a good idea for any member of Congress and is certainly not recommended. It was a "fly-out" day, and we were all headed home. The president offered me to travel with him to an event where he was speaking. The trip would have required me to fly with him to another state, then make additional flight arrangements from that location back to Atlanta. Though inconvenient, I should have accepted his invitation for obvious reasons. Opportunities like that are exceedingly uncommon. But I declined because of activities scheduled in the district, not to mention the fact that I was just ready to get home. Nonetheless, as soon as the words of refusal left my mouth, I immediately knew I had made a colossal blunder. And indeed, it was. It took almost forever for another opportunity on Air Force One to present itself. That decision was dumb!

Not only were the experiences of traveling with President Trump remarkable, but it was also a privilege to be with him at rallies and in other settings. His exceptional ability to work with a crowd, as well as his capacity to connect on a personal basis with individuals, was astonishing. I had several opportunities to witness his skills in operation and was always amazed by his talents. I also had several opportunities to be with him on stage and, in a few instances, to speak briefly alongside him. Obviously, the mass crowds were there to see him, but being a recipient of their "spillover" energy was an experience of its own.

Trump was even gracious enough to invite me to his golf club in Bedminster as well as Mar-a-Lago several times. While there, we engaged in deep policy discussion while enjoying delicious meals served in palatial halls. He held several fundraisers for my campaign that invigorated my race both financially and morally. His open door was an incredible kindness he didn't need to offer but chose to anyway.

Another highlight for me, as would be the case for any American, involved meetings in the White House. I was blessed to have many of those meetings, mostly about policy discussions or issues the Freedom Caucus was working on, but every visit to the White House was an extreme honor. On one such occasion, President Trump gave me a ceremonial "key" to the White House. Knowing that such a profound treasure is rarely given, it obviously commands a place of prominence in my office today. I have so many fond memories of time spent with the president; I found him to be a very gracious and thoughtful person.

I was also blessed to have many opportunities to meet with leaders from around the world. My wife was born in England, so my conversation and picture with U.K. Prime Minister Theresa May will always be remembered and cherished on a personal level. I would invariably pinch myself to affirm the reality of moments like that; they were, indeed, fantastic occasions. Prior to Congress, these were meetings I could only dream about, and the fact that they had become a reality was beyond wonder. One of the most prized for me was meeting with Israeli Prime Minister Benjamin Netanyahu in the Israeli Knesset. Israel has always held a special place in my heart, and Netanyahu has always been a highly respected leader for me. On this occasion, I was part of a congressional delegation (Co-Del) that was sponsored by the Oversight Committee and its chairman, Jason Chaffetz. This Co-Del focused on visits to a host of different U.S. military bases around the world. We had warm encounters with military personnel, participated in incredible briefings pertaining to military preparedness and national security, and saw some of our unbelievable weapon systems and technology. Along the way, we went to Israel and there, had the opportunity to affirm our national support for Israel and to hear directly from Prime Minister Netanyahu about some of the challenges his country was experiencing. It was a meeting I will never forget. I later received a letter of gratitude from him, thanking us for coming and visiting with him. Of course, that letter hangs on my office wall today.

There are so many experiences to relay, but one item that continues to be in the news almost every day is the southern border. As a member of Congress, I was extremely involved with trying to protect our southern border, both by legislation and personal engagement. As a member of the Border Caucus, I was determined to gain as much information as possible. Thus, I thought it prudent to personally visit the border and witness the situation myself. Over the course of a couple of years, I visited all nine sectors of our southern border and experienced first-hand the true invasion that is taking place. I met with border agents and local sheriffs, and even had dinner with a family whose property is on the border. We visited many detention centers and border headquarters, receiving "briefs" and having conversations, both with those who had illegally entered the United States as well as our agents who were working against unwinnable odds. More often than I can count, my eyes watched illegal crossings in real time, during the daytime as well as late at night. I saw the filth left behind by "coyotes" who were trafficking both people and drugs. And I witnessed the sickening remains of horrible crimes they had committed. It was gruesome to behold. One could only imagine the unspeakable abuse that had been inflicted upon their victims. The abhorrent odor of human sweat and excrement, combined with leftover drugs and trash, is still vivid to my mental nostrils.

I wanted to see and experience everything possible at the border. It was part of my commitment to gain knowledge and information. Frankly, I wish all Americans could see the things that I saw. If that could happen, the people of this country would most certainly demand that our borders be secured. On a daily basis, thousands of people are flooding across the borderline. Large numbers of them have criminal histories, many are involved in drug and human trafficking, and an unknown number are carriers of various diseases. It is a situation that should never happen in the United States and is one that could easily be prevented with a simple commitment to doing so.

Regarding travel, there are many opportunities for members of Congress, both domestically and internationally. Perhaps the most haunting and perilous occurrence, one that I will never forget, involved a train. The various railcars were filled with GOP members on January 17, 2018, as we journeyed at a high speed and on our way to a conference retreat in West Virginia. Suddenly, an enormous impact rocked the train as we crashed into a large truck that was attempting to cross the tracks. The collision was immense, and it resulted in the death of one individual inside the truck. Honestly, it is downright amazing that two other individuals in the vehicle survived the massive impact and carnage. Equally remarkable, the train did not derail, and no one on board was seriously harmed, although a few suffered minor injuries and pain due to a severe tumble they took. Indeed, unforgettable!

And speaking of bereavement, I will never forget receiving a phone call early in the morning on November 19th, 2015, informing me that my mom had just passed away. I was in my first year as the representative from GA-10, and although she had been ill, the news of her passing was devastating. Mom had played a vital role in my life and in fact, she had personally led me to Christ when I was 13 years old. I was emotionally dazed and shaken by the call. That day we were scheduled to vote on the SAFE Act, which was legislation concerning Syrian and Iraqi refugees coming into the United States. The bill was a consequential response to a recent attack in Paris, and there were grave concerns that ISIL terrorists might attempt to infiltrate the United States through the refugee program. Among other things, the SAFE Act required the FBI, the Department of Homeland Security, and the director of national intelligence to boost background checks and investigations for refugees from

Syria or Iraq, for fear that there might be extremists trying to enter our homeland for nefarious reasons. Obviously, my heart was broken that day, and more than anything, all I desperately wanted was to catch the first flight home. On the other hand, although most people would probably understand the situation, I was mindful that the 10th District had elected me to represent them to the best of my ability, despite personal struggles. Mom had always been passionate about current news and the need for leaders to stand strong amid changing times. I kept telling myself that she would want me to vote before going home.

Within minutes, the daily grind in Washington was underway, and I found myself numbly walking down the hallway for a meeting when I unexpectedly ran into Mark Meadows. As was his custom, he asked how I was doing, and I informed him that my mom had passed away a short time earlier. He reacted tartly, "Why are you here? Go home!" I replied, "Mark, we are voting on an important bill today, and I know my mom would want me to stay and vote." He silently looked at me for several seconds, and then began to nod his head as if sharing in my pain and struggle. He sincerely communicated a like-minded sense of understanding, and then he said, "Jody, I will be praying for you today." He will never fully comprehend how that brief encounter was used by God to provide me an extra dose of peace and strength for the day. I will always be grateful for that encounter. Following the vote, arrangements were made for me to depart as quickly as possible. Upon arriving home, I was comforted to learn that my mom had passed away with a smile on her face and with one arm raised in the air, as if being greeted by someone and being welcomed home. Indeed, I'm confident that is exactly what she experienced!

As you probably know, Mark Meadows was one of the founding members of the House Freedom Caucus and served as its
second president. He was an outstanding leader but made a
national name for himself when he challenged the speakership of
John Boehner by filing a motion to vacate the chair. For doing so,
Mark endured an enormous amount of antagonism. But it was
the right thing to do, and history has certainly substantiated that
fact. There is no doubt in my mind that Boehner needed to go.

For one thing, he seemed always to lean leftward on issues
that urgently needed a true conservative stance. But further, he
ruled with an iron fist, and there were frequent, and sometimes
severe, consequences for not "falling in line" with his leadership expectations. In fact, I had not been in Congress for three
months before ads were run against me in GA-10. Negative
billboards and radio ads seemed to be everywhere! I was told
that Boehner was behind those ads because he did not like the
way I had voted on a particular issue. The district ads were his
attempt to intimidate me into compliance. This type of behavior was common. He also made sure that I, along with other
like-minded conservatives, were unable to attain D.C. funding
for our campaigns. Obviously, we were too conservative for the
establishment, and thus he attempted to inflict political harm,
both in the district and within the D.C. community.

To be sure, Boehner was not the only speaker or high-level
leader who demanded members to yield to their authority. In
fact, for all practical purposes, having to relinquish one's voting card was virtually expected if you wanted certain committee
assignments, fundraisers, or bills that you wanted to be voted on
the floor. I remember vividly when Leader Kevin McCarthy had
me kicked off the House Armed Services Committee because I

had voted against him for speaker. It had taken nearly two years of work on my part to get on HASC (House Armed Services Committee), and because of my vote, he removed me after only six months of being selected. But that's the D.C. way, and that's why people despise Washington. The manner of doing business in D.C. has been so twisted for so long that it is now understood to be standard operating procedure. It truly is a "swamp."

That is why I have the utmost respect and admiration for members of the Freedom Caucus. As a group, they refuse to cave in to such abhorrent demands and expectations. Under the leadership and example of Jim Jordan, Mark Meadows, and others, HFC (House Freedom Caucus) became a powerful block in the Halls of Congress. Being a group of political warriors committed to doing the right thing rather than going along to get along, they became one of the most influential voices for the American people and a dominant force within the House of Representatives. One of the aspects of Congress that I miss the most are the HFC meetings. Unlike most of the other caucuses and political gatherings, the Freedom Caucus met to discuss genuine strategies for maintaining American liberties and protecting our constitutional republic. To this day, I stay in touch with many of those great friends and wish them all continued success in their valiant efforts.

Another amazing part of Congress, and something I miss greatly, was the ability to participate in important hearings. I emphatically valued serving on the Oversight Committee. It had jurisdiction over any area of our federal government, wherever there was waste, fraud, or abuse. As you can imagine, it was and continues to be a very busy committee! From the IRS targeting conservatives, to corruption within the FBI and the infamous "false dossier" and "Russian hoax," there were hundreds of critical issues that Oversight confronted. It was an extremely fulfilling place to serve because it was one of the few committees in Congress that could move the needle. For example, when IRS Director John Koskinen testified before us, it became evident that corruption was deep within his agency and the tentacles of vice reached all the way to the top. During my time of questioning him, I called on him to resign. To my great satisfaction, within a short time following that hearing, he announced his forthcoming retirement. There were several other occasions when we were able to root out corruption and save the American people from inefficient and duplicitous government operations. It was very rewarding, indeed.

Obviously, one of the most incredible aspects of Congress is having the opportunity to write legislation and to have it signed into law. I had four such pieces. In addition, there were multiple bills that I helped get across the finish line for other colleagues. Of course, there were many pieces of legislation that never saw the light of day or that died in the Senate. That reality is merely part of the arduous process of legislating. But having had the opportunity to develop and move legislation is almost beyond conception. And besides lawmaking, there were many hundreds of opportunities to help constituents with federal issues that were impacting their lives, offer nominations for outstanding young men and women to one of our service academies, or advance major projects within the district.

One example is Kettle Creek Battlefield, on the outskirts of Washington, Georgia, in Wilkes County. Its history dates to the Revolutionary War. Though not well known, Kettle Creek represents a turning point for the American Revolution as it was the first significant Patriot victory in Georgia's backcountry. Savannah and much of Georgia had already fallen into British control. But on February 14, 1779, a small group of freedom lovers defeated John Boyd and his troops, sending shockwaves down both sides of the conflict, and "the rest is history." For nearly 100 years, different Representatives had sought to gain recognition for Kettle Creek, all to no avail. But through intense efforts by my staff, the Kettle Creek community, former UGA Coach Vince Dooley, and hard work on the Natural Resources Committee, we were successful in obtaining official recognition for Kettle Creek Battlefield as an affiliated unit of the National Parks Service, after six long years of struggle. The joy associated with such an accomplishment is genuine. America must protect her history, and for the national freedoms that were secured because of the patriots of Kettle Creek, it was worth having an enduring, but successful, congressional battle.

Perhaps the most meaningful victory our office ever experienced came from our efforts to rescue masses of people out of Afghanistan when President Biden pulled our forces out in 2021. There were thousands of Americans who were stranded there, along with an unknown number of individuals who were not U.S. citizens but who were strong and vocal advocates. As a result of the withdrawal, they were now at great risk of life and had been abandoned by the United States. There was no way out of the country, and many of them faced certain death if captured. Unfortunately, the U.S. State Department was of little to no help at all. In fact, it contributed enormously to the problem. It was slow to respond to our calls, frequently provided us with inaccurate or misleading information, and at times seemed to deliberately obstruct rescue opportunities. Ours was certainly not the only office working diligently to save people, but we were one of the top tiers. Under the leadership of my district director, Jessica Hayes, a team was formed, and we worked almost 24/7 for weeks on end. Yes, we cried buckets of tears for those we could not save and celebrated beyond imagination for those we were able to liberate. Literally, an entire book could (and probably should) be written about this horrendous situation and the heroic efforts of many people who were as stealthy as ghosts, but who produced one miracle after another, and the untold hours that were committed to bring about encouragement, support, and aid to those forsaken souls.

As of this writing, over two years after the fact, our team is still successfully assisting and transporting people at risk out of Afghanistan and into safety and freedom. Looking back, that was one of the most intense times of my life. It was with immense emotions that I was personally able to meet and converse with a few of those rescued individuals and families. Their profound and heartfelt indebtedness to the rescue efforts was something that my memory would never abandon. Further, their love for political freedom and safety is difficult to explain to someone who has not witnessed it at such a deep and personal level. Most people cannot fathom the rich devotion they have for America. It is only appropriate for me to acknowledge with extreme gratitude: Jessica Hayes, Tim Reitz, Keri Gardner, Beth Goolsby, Lauren Sanders, Edward Shelor, the many organized prayer supporters, and those who served as our underground informants and rescue teams. God bless each of you heroes—thank you!

I am frequently asked, "How difficult was it to exercise your faith in Washington, D.C.?" To begin with, it's natural for people to imagine what a new job might be like and to anticipate what it might entail. I certainly did that regarding Congress. Among other things, prior to being an official member, I fully anticipated being a "loner" regarding my faith. But much to my surprise, I found that Christianity is alive and well in Congress; at least, that was my experience within the Republican conference. There were many Bible studies and prayer meetings available for members to attend, and virtually every meeting that we held as a conference started with a prayer. Consequently, it was not long before I offered a weekly Bible study in my office, and it was well attended until Covid prohibited such meetings. All this is to say that my ability to live according to my faith was not hindered. In fact, most members of Congress on both sides of the aisle knew that I had been a pastor, and they respected that fact. Frankly, it seems to me that the First Amendment is under greater attack throughout the heartland of America rather than within the halls of Congress. Time will not allow me to share the many occasions I had to practice my faith, but there were many, from praying with media celebrities in the hallway to speaking biblical truth in hearings. I would say that with all the negative and dark aspects of "The Swamp," the freedom to speak and live in accordance with my Christian beliefs was not a problem.

Again, there are so many opportunities and experiences that are unique to Congress. Under no other profession would I be allowed to land by helicopter and tour oil refineries in the Gulf of Mexico? Never would I have attended State of the Union addresses or enjoyed a casual dinner with the vice president in his personal residence. Never would I have enjoyed sitting in a

private suite with my daughter and the president of the United
States, watching UGA play in the national championship foot-
ball game. No other profession would have allowed me to speak
my views to the American people through an untold number of
media outlets. And because members of Congress are given a
virtual key to the city of Washington, D.C., I have been able to
use that honor to take our grandchildren to see some amazing
tours and places.

But most of all, being a member of the United States House of
Representatives provided me the indescribable honor, for a brief
time in my life, to represent and serve the 10th District, the state
of Georgia, and the United States as a whole.

Through many ups and downs in my life, I sought every day
to be a congressman who operated out of genuine integrity of
heart and selflessness. I learned, on an extremely deep level, that
character is of utmost importance. I was raised to be honest,
but not until those values are tested and stretched to the limit
is the certainty of character discovered. No doubt, I have many
cherished memories of my time in Congress, but the ones that
linger the most profoundly are those that were tough. It was the
times when seemingly alone in a frying pan, the easy way would
have been to capitulate. Those experiences serve as a strong
and daily voice, calling me to ever take the "road less traveled."
Without holding steadfast to convictions in the face of tremendous pressure, without guarding the heart against the wiles of
waywardness, and without making perpetual decisions to walk
uprightly, then failure would be most certain. I am keenly aware
that within all of us, myself included, is the capacity to fall. And
God knows, I don't want that horrible conclusion to my life's
legacy. As Proverbs 25:26 says, "A righteous man who falters

before the wicked is like a murky spring and a polluted well." It's hard to stay pure, but falling to the deception of compromise is worse. When the pressure goes up, so must true character. As the world is getting more and more off-center as relating to right and wrong, every effort must be made to guard our hearts. There are no shortcuts—integrity matters!

5

Democrats Push for Election Reform

Show yourself in all respects to be a model of good works, and
in your teaching show integrity, dignity, and sound speech
that cannot be condemned, so that an opponent may be put to
shame, having nothing evil to say about us.

—TITUS 2:7–8

The future of this Republic is in the hands of the American
voter.

—PRESIDENT DWIGHT D. EISENHOWER

S OME PEOPLE HAVE ASKED me, "What makes you an author-ity on election integrity?" It's a fair question, and to be hon-est, I'm confident there are others who are much more qualified than I am. But there is no question this issue became a major emphasis for me in Congress and has continued to be one since I left. Although election integrity was not particularly on my radar prior to 2020, it became a fight that I was somewhat forced into. For me, the battle line was drawn during my time on the House Oversight Committee. Democrats started pushing for election reforms that, in my opinion, would destroy election integrity rather than secure it. And the more they spoke about their plans, the more passionate they became, and the more concerned I became. Eventually, it was undeniable that they were on a pathway to radically change the election process and to federalize it in such a way as to give Democrats a major advantage at the ballot box nationwide. This quickly became an issue that could not be ignored, and I stepped into the arena. Allow me to provide some historical and chronological context.

To the best of our determination, it was December 2019 when the Covid-19 virus likely leaked from a lab in Wuhan, China. Shortly thereafter, on January 15, 2020, an individual from Washington state returned to the United States after visiting with family in Wuhan. Because the virus was beginning to get some media attention, on the 19th of January, he checked into a hospital due to symptoms he was experiencing. For safety reasons, he thought it best to be tested. On January 20th, he was confirmed positive for the Covid virus, and he became America's first case. I recall hearing the news. It created a sense of uncertainty and trepidation as to what this might mean for our nation. The news of a potential outbreak of coronavirus seemed to sound an alarm within the national medical community. However, the average citizen was paying little attention to the likelihood of a conceivable pandemic, let alone a mass overreach of government into our lives that would soon occur through mandatory shutdowns, vaccine requirements, and the like.

It was within this background of Covid-19 that Democrats began fervently discussing the need for changes in election

laws. The coronavirus became their reason to demand immediate action. Less than a week following the first coronavirus
case in the United States on January 26, we had an Oversight
hearing about "voter suppression." During the hearing, Rep.
Gerry Connolly (VA-11) passionately claimed America was suffering from an "epidemic of voter suppression laws." He used
this catchphrase to describe the urgent need to change election
laws and to do so *now*. Although it did not fully register with me
at the time, I nonetheless found it interesting that he used "epidemic" to describe election suppression less than one week after
the first reported case. Already, the national news media was
painting a dismal picture of a potential Covid epidemic on the
horizon. Indeed, it was a curious choice of words that Connolly
used. In the same hearing, Jamie Raskin (MD-8) admitted that
Democrats were "fighting to reconstruct the Voting Rights Act."
In this Oversight hearing, the Democrats were clearly driving
a message, and they did not waiver from their mission. To say
they were all unified would be a significant understatement.
They were obviously setting the political table for a bigger push.

In their attempt to convince America that voter suppression
was a serious problem, they used Georgia as "Exhibit A." Stacey
Abrams, as you probably recall, had lost her bid to be governor of Georgia and blamed voter suppression as the reason for
her loss. In fact, she never conceded defeat but instead used her
political failure as an opportunity to declare widespread voter
suppression in the state. (It is interesting that when a Democrat
challenges an election, it is considered a legitimate claim and
worthy of serious investigation, but if a Republican does so, it
is considered a "threat" to democracy. The double standard is
both unfair and alarming.) I am from Georgia and know the

state well. Our election laws are generous and fair, certainly not suppressive. Sure, there are always things that can be improved, but for the most part, our state elections have been considered secure throughout my lifetime. Nonetheless, using the undercurrent created by Stacey Abrams, Democrats pushed their narrative of voter suppression, and I began to push back. As I painfully endured the Oversight hearing that day, the "spin" utilized by my Democratic colleagues was frightful in its effectiveness. They were striking a political nerve and were determined to take full advantage of the opportunity.

No less than three weeks following the first reported case in the United States, on February 6, 2020, *Politico* ran an article, "Democrats Launch Massive Legal Campaign on Voting Ahead of 2020."[1] Written by Nolan D. McCaskill, it revealed how millions of dollars were being spent at the direction of Democrats, to fight against various states for performing voter registration purges and implementing voter ID requirements. They were also attempting to challenge various rules regarding signature matches and ballot orders. These were all routine and widely accepted features needed for election reliability and had been taking place for decades. What did these have to do with Covid, and why the urgent push from Democrats to abandon these necessities immediately? While the rest of America was beginning to focus on an emerging epidemic, congressional Democrats were gearing up for the 2020 elections, and Covid became the horse they would ride to gain momentum for their cause and to heave guilt upon anyone who disagreed with their demands.

Interestingly, during the January 26 Oversight hearing that I referenced, Democrats started mentioning a piece of legislation that would soon become their signature election reform bill.

They referred to HR. 1, and almost immediately it rose to the surface as a priority for the Pelosi-controlled Democratic Party. I will deal more with the details of the legislation later, but it is a horrible proposal so far as election security is concerned.

On March 11, Oversight held another hearing entitled "Coronavirus Preparedness and Response." By this time, multiple news outlets had started broadcasting the attempts that were underway. On April 9, for example, the *New York Post* ran an opinion piece, "Democrats Trying to use Coronavirus Crisis to Rewrite US Election Law."[2] In the article, David Harsanyi declared that Massachusetts Sen. Elizabeth Warren had already proposed legislation to require mandatory automatic and same-day registration, ending voter ID requirements, and a minimum of 15 days for early and mail voting.

Looking back, I am filled with many questions that will probably never be answered. The Democrats, in what seemed like an eerie foreknowledge of the pandemic's future impact, were forcefully and effectively moving their agenda for election reform while Republicans and the rest of the country were simply trying to wrap their heads around the early stages of a pandemic. As if employing a premeditated strategy, Democrats were broadly unified in their messaging, and virtually able to forecast what the virus was going to do. Did they know something the rest of us did not know? How were they able to wield so much influence, even beyond D.C., in altering election laws so rapidly, and in so many states? Indeed, there are many unanswered questions.

Like most people, the pandemic raised concerns for my family and loved ones. And like most Americans, I was frequently distracted by the daily bombardment of seeing minute-by-minute news reports about the spread of Covid and how to be protected. At the same time, I was bewildered as the government began shutting down "non-essential" businesses, giving orders for stay-at-home lockdowns, etc. Congress itself was feeling pressure to address the situation and to be proactive. As a matter of record, I voted "no" on most all the Covid spending proposals because, first, we are already in serious financial trouble with the national debt, and secondly, deep inside, something did not seem right with the entire scenario. There was too much political debris swirling around that seemed to create an environment for opportunism rather than a rational reply to a healthcare emergency. But perhaps the biggest concern I had at the time was watching with great suspicion as my Democratic colleagues took giant strides toward controlling the upcoming election, be it through legislation or by simply guiding the narrative. Among other things, they were effectively convincing the nation that a pandemic would cause people to be fearful of leaving their homes to cast a vote, or perhaps lockdowns would prohibit them from doing so. Their solution was to mandate distribution of ballots to every home with little-to-no verification as to their eligibility to vote. But Covid was not the only ingredient for change, it was the "tip of the iceberg" regarding a broader message. They were indeed making huge advances.

Stacey Abrams's Voter Suppression Claim

Stacey Abrams made numerous claims of voter suppression following her defeat, and the enticement of her appeal produced a textbook opportunity and rallying cry for Democrats. Her assertion generated a powerful emotional dynamism because it was a call to end racial discrimination at the ballot box and to guarantee election justice for all. And whether nor not her claims were true did not matter, no one could possibly oppose her plea for fairness in elections. A prevailing narrative was being shaped. Her repetitious accusations drew widespread sympathy and provided a "perfect storm" for Democrats to canter. As though in rehearsed unison, they began beating a drum and demanding change. The messengers were emotionally and ethnically charged, and the media helped validate the frenzy that was being generated. "Truth" took a back seat to verbal passion and a steady assertion of serious allegations. Instinctively, Democrats knew that if they could win the rhetorical battle, they could change the minds of Americans and potentially attain election reform. As I witnessed firsthand, their message became a formidable influence with Washington Democrats, and it became an occasion to showcase Georgia as "proof" of problematic nationwide voter suppression.

My congressional district, GA-10, consisted of some 25 counties, mostly rural. One of those, Jefferson County, was named in honor of the Declaration of Independence's chief author and third president of the United States, Thomas Jefferson. The county, established on February 20, 1796, boasts a rich history and today has a modest population of about 15,000. Jefferson County is a friendly place where few crimes are committed and where God and family are still held in high regard. Louisville, the county seat, is a quaint Southern town, and the residents like it that way. But everything instantly changed one October morning in 2018. They were thrust into a media cyclone filled with ugly accusations and charges. At least temporarily, Jefferson County became a living example of the Democrats' insistence for election reform. Like it or not, the county became a poster

child for voter suppression. Let me explain the seditious screen-
play that appears to have transpired.

I vividly recall the panic-stricken voice on the other end of
my phone on Monday, October 15, 2018. Calling for help and
advice was a local official who was terrified by the sudden media
attention and serious allegations troubling the otherwise quiet
community. He said that management personnel from the local
Leisure Center, a city-run activities complex for seniors, were
being accused of voter suppression, and the left-wing media
was wreaking havoc. As the story would unfold over the next
few days, it became suspiciously curious as to the validity of the
assertions.

Georgia's early voting was to begin Monday, October 15,
and among many races that would be decided, by far the most
notable was the governor's race between Stacey Abrams (D) and
Brian Kemp (R). On Sunday night, October 14, at 10:23 p.m.,
Diane Evans, committee chair of the local Democratic Party,
wrote an email to Tammie Bennett, director of the Jefferson
County Leisure Center. The message requested permission for
Evans and a group called Black Voters Matter (BVM) to meet
with seniors *the next morning* at 11:00 a.m. for the purpose of
encouraging them to vote. The email also stated the desire to
encourage seniors to attend an event with the Democratic candidate for lieutenant governor, Sarah Riggs Amico, which was to
be held at the local bistro at 1 p.m. the same day.

Although BVM claims to be bipartisan, nothing could be
further from the truth. Again, the email was sent by the head
of the local Democratic Party, and BVM is known to be an
organization that helps Democratic candidates. In fact, BVM
boasted often about the huge role it played in helping Democrat

Doug Jones win the U.S. Senate race in Alabama a year earlier. No doubt, BVM was in Jefferson County to try and influence Democratic voters, which is why they were promoting the meet-and-greet with Ms. Amico. The request was most definitely not intended to promote a bipartisan event. Further, the method Evans used to gain permission was sneaky at best. Sending an email at 10:30 p.m. on Sunday for a meeting the next morning is either a gross lack of planning or an attempt to be sly. As a rule, people in Jefferson County are not reading or responding to emails at that time of night. In fact, most were probably in bed. The request was indeed conniving, not to mention unrealistic. The chicanery is further revealed by the fact that Evans also contacted one of the cofounders of BVM, Cliff Albright, informing him that she had emailed the Leisure Center's director, but "had not heard back." Obviously, she failed to mention the timing of her email.

Another interesting detail that was not mentioned by the media firestorm involved a conversation between County Commissioner Gonice Davis and Diane Evans, which took place on Sunday morning. In an interview with an ABC affiliate, News Channel 6, he said the conversation with Evans had been about a "religious organization" whose intent was to help seniors who needed resources following hurricane Michael, which had been downgraded to a tropical storm when it came through Georgia on October 10. The most interesting aspect of his interview was that nothing in the conversation with Evans was connected to voting or putting seniors on a bus to vote.[3] Assuming BVM was the "religious organization" Evans referenced, it would soon become abundantly clear that BVM was neither religious nor was it concerned about helping seniors after the storm.

Nonetheless, the next day Diane Evans and BVM were allowed to visit and speak at the Leisure Center upon permission by the director, Tammie Bennett. Following a brief program that included an appeal to vote, a group of Black seniors, approximately 50 in number, were invited to tour the BVM bus. Once on the bus, someone suggested the group should go vote, right then. I am not clear as to who contacted Director Bennett at that time, but upon being informed that the bus driver intended to leave the premises, Bennett objected and promptly intervened. She informed the driver that BVM had not been vetted and they could not leave without proper authorization. Also, the Leisure Center offered free transportation to the voting site, as frequently as needed. The whole scenario appeared to be a setup. In fact, as the seniors were coming off the bus, certain individuals were already prepared and poised with video cameras, filming the elderly people being "forced" off the bus and denied the right to vote. Almost immediately, the Leisure Center heard chimes of "voter suppression," and now there was "video footage" of them coming off the bus, as evidence.[4] Within no time, Left-leaning media began covering the story with depictions of cruel, racially motivated "proof" of voter suppression. The panicked phone call that I received from Adam Brett, a county official, was in response to all the negative press and misleading information that was being circulated. Among the first to twist the story and distort the truth was ThinkProgress, a staunch left-wing organization. At 12:55 p.m. on Monday, October 15, literally within minutes of the ordeal, it posted an article entitled, "UPDATE: This is live voter suppression: Black Voters Matter blocked from taking seniors to vote," complete with the video recordings. It is hard to believe such an article could have been posted so quickly without it having been planned, and having personnel "planted" beforehand to capture a video recording.[5] No reporter could have interviewed witnesses, written an editorial, obtained video recordings, and posted an article so fast without first having someone present at the event, anticipating a story to unfold, and prepared with video equipment and pen in hand.

On Tuesday, immediately following the conflict, the city of Louisville received a letter from the NAACP Legal Defense and Educational Fund. Signed by Leah Aden, the organization's deputy director of litigation, they demanded a thorough investigation into the incident and claimed the city might have violated several laws by potentially enabling voter intimidation. As the external pressure mounted and negative media coverage spread, angst among city officials also dramatically increased. The simple question was: Did the Leisure Center suppress voters? The answer is clear, they absolutely did not. First, as a matter policy: They do not sponsor or host political events, which the BVM gathering clearly was. The Center's purpose is to provide a hub for seniors to gather and mingle, not to accommodate an atmosphere of potential disharmony through divisive political meetings. Second, the BVM organization had not been vetted, and no one at the Leisure Center knew who they were. To allow an unknown group (BVM) to leave with a bus full of attendees could conceivably result in legal action against the city had there been an accident en route or some other nefarious plan.

Another part of the story worth mentioning is that months before this significant day, my office had planned and organized an event for veterans to be held at the Leisure Center facility, on October 27. So following the happenings that took place on October 15 and statements from the Leisure Center's management that they do not host political meetings, many on the Left argued that my upcoming event was political and therefore the Center should disinvite me or rescind its claim of being nonpolitical. After many conversations and amid great apprehension from various stakeholders, I was very proud of the city and Leisure Center for the way they handled the immense pressure. To be sure, they would have loved to cancel our veterans' meeting, but gratefully, they did not. Instead, they moved forward with the event and added security in case demonstrators tried to create disorder. Fortunately, there were no problems with dissenters. The event was a great success, and we had an effective time helping a significant number of American heroes.

But to be clear, my event was not political, it was official. As a member of Congress, we routinely provide informational meetings throughout the district for veterans and many other groups. That's part of the job! And when on official business, we are strictly forbidden from speaking about or engaging in "political" activities. To do so could result in an ethics violation, which can be a very serious matter. So we were then, as always, extremely careful not to mix politics with official business. Nonetheless, the fact that our meeting was scheduled became a source of consternation for some. Even Snopes, the professed fact-checking experts, provided misleading information about my visit.[6] The truth is, we provided a free continental breakfast and a turkey giveaway in appreciation to our nation's heroes. Further, we offered help to veterans on issues ranging from housing, VA benefits, suicide prevention, filing claims, employment, and more. There was never a word spoken about an election nor was there an appeal for votes. We were on official business, period. What we did was massively different from the event performed by BVM, which was led by the local Democratic committee chair in conjunction with an openly political organization, both of whom were soliciting votes for their party. And most unfortunately, out of the political scene they created came an opportunity for a "messaging point" that Democrats fully exploited to their advantage: vote suppression.

We are all familiar with the political phrase from Rahm Emanuel, former chief of staff for President Obama, "Don't let a good crisis go to waste." It is amazing how many embrace that philosophy. Interestingly, Stacey Abrams arrived for a rally in Louisville on October 17, two days after the debacle, and attempted to get as much mileage as possible from the voter suppression accusation. Using the depiction of Black voters being forced off a bus and being disallowed to vote, she encouraged voters in the town to "fight voter suppression." She declared, "My goal is to make certain that every person be able to cast their vote. . . . Even if there are obstacles, we have to recognize that those obstacles are only permanent if we don't fight them."[7]

As is often the case, the truth eventually prevailed, but not until maximum damage had already been inflicted. That memorable day in Jefferson County, Georgia, was soon acknowledged as a mere miscommunication rather than voter suppression. However, the ability for Democrats to capitalize on the assertions had been completed. Characterizing this community as participating in organized and premeditated voter suppression, be it intentional or accidental, had been successful, and it drew national attention. Yes, the truth eventually came out, but it was too late. Georgia was viewed nationally as a state inundated with racially motivated voter suppression. It was amid this backdrop that Democrats in D.C., specifically those serving on the House

Oversight Committee, made relentless characterizations portraying Georgia as being discriminatory against Black voters. This mantra became another reason to demand immediate election reform.

I think the average American, upon looking at the facts of this situation, would be appalled. Whether the events that took place in Louisville, Georgia, on October 15, 2018, consisted of authentic miscommunication on the part of city officials or a planned strategy from Democrats, the fact that it was not publicly and nationally corrected when the truth came out is unacceptable. This occurrence must be looked upon and reflected upon for what it is, an attack on election integrity. I understand that politics is dirty business, but elections must remain intellectually "sacred" if they are to have any chance of remaining secure. Never should elections be cheapened to the extent of becoming a political tool for the purpose of an advancing a political agenda, or as it seems in this case, to advance legislation for the purpose of giving one party an advantage over the other.

To be clear, as it relates to elections, I am not primarily concerned about who wins. Ultimately, that is a secondary issue. My concern, as should be the same with all freedom-loving Americans, is whether an election was a fair representation of the voice and will of the people. If elections cease to be honest, America will cease to be free. As such, to paint a picture of voter suppression in such a deceptive fashion as what happened in Jefferson County, Georgia, is playing with the potential disintegration of the people's voice. May this example highlight the need for greater protections. Never should we allow a superficial crisis to be created, and then "fix" it with legislation, for no other reason but selfish and political advancement.

6

A Phone Call: Deceptive Silence

He who is faithful in what is least is faithful also in much; and he who is unjust in what is least is unjust also in much."

—LUKE 16:10

Whoever is careless with the truth in small matters cannot be trusted in important affairs.

—ALBERT EINSTEIN

I N 2020, UNDER THE guise of the Covid emergency, Democrats in D.C. were aggressively trying to enact election reforms for their benefit. As I have already described, while the rest of the nation was bracing for safety amid a pandemic, Democrats seemed focused on the November election and seeking ways to tilt the scales their way. For this reason, the Republican members of the Georgia delegation deemed it prudent to call our Secretary of State, Brad Raffensperger, and warn him of the attempts of the Democrats in Washington, D.C., and the possibility that their efforts could impact Georgia. Rumors were already swirling that Stacey Abrams would be acting in cahoots with other Democrats and would attempt to significantly change the state's election laws. Perhaps our Secretary of State was aware of the rumors and potential threat, or maybe he was not. Either way, it was a matter that our delegation decided could not be assumed or ignored, as the plausible risk was too great.

So in March 2020, a phone call was arranged. To my recollection, all Republican members from the Georgia delegation were present. On the other end of the phone line was Georgia's Secretary of State, Brad Raffensperger. Whether or not he had an attorney or staff member on the call, I do not know. But the lead spokesmen from our Georgia delegation were representatives Buddy Carter (GA-1) and Drew Ferguson (GA-3). Lasting approximately 20 minutes, the conversation was pleasant and cordial, although no significant commitments were made by Secretary Raffensperger. Instead, he seemed to be in "listening mode" only and did not divert from that posture. Although representatives Carter and Ferguson were the most vocal, the primary and unified message given to the secretary was an urgent plea to not send absentee ballots to everyone on Georgia's voter registration file. Of all the rumors being floated, that one seemed to be most egregious and concerning. The voter file was known to be inaccurate to some extent, and many believed it to be incorrect by as much as 10 percent or more. In Georgia, state law requires maintenance and improvement of the voter file every other year, on nonelection years. Being a rapidly growing state due to its beauty, climate, and favorable environment for business, it is impossible to maintain accurate files by viewing it only once, every other year. We had credible reason to believe Stacey Abrams would push for absentee ballots to be mailed to the entire voter registration file, using the pandemic as justification for immediate changes to the election process. So we urged Mr. Raffensperger to be cognizant of her plans, as well as the overall strategy that was seemingly unfolding among Democrats in D.C. We urged him to be aware and to not give in if a proposal developed.

Although he never mentioned it during our phone conversation, we found out about 10 months after the fact that he and Stacey Abrams had already made some sort of deal about two weeks prior to our call with him. In many ways, the "cake" to transform Georgia's election laws had already been baked, and we were uninformed, even after personally speaking with the secretary. Looking back on the call, I now realize why he was in "listening mode" only—he did not want to let us know that the decision had already been made. It appears that Stacey did in fact request live absentee ballots be sent to the entire Georgia voter registration file. As a matter of compromise, an agreement was reached whereby a "request" for an absentee ballot would be mailed to everyone on the file, not an actual ballot. That might be a marginal improvement, but still a disastrous decision.

Beyond the obvious practicality of this being an exceedingly unwise decision, one major problem is that the Secretary of State does not have authorization to make or change laws individually. The legislative body makes laws, not the executive branch nor specifically the Secretary of State. But in this circumstance, it appears that by assuming emergency powers due to Covid, without approval from the Georgia General Assembly, a unilateral decision was made by the secretary to mail absentee ballot requests to every registered voter in Georgia, without the file being up to date and accurate. According to the *Atlanta Journal*, Georgia had approximately 7.6 million registered voters in 2020.[1] As time would prove and as we warned on the phone call in March, this decision was a catastrophic mistake. Georgia would soon experience absolute mayhem in the upcoming November election and would attract the attention and scrutiny of the entire nation. What a senseless embarrassment to the state and a mockery so far as election integrity is concerned. Georgia had never done such a thing, and by mailing an absentee ballot request to every registered voter, without significant verification as to their existence in the state or overall eligibility, would potentially open wide the doors for fraudulent activity and overwhelm a system that was not designed or prepared to manage over 1.4 million absentee ballots that would be returned. With virtually no voter identification in place, how could we know or prove that the ballots came from a legally registered Georgia voter?

It was with that phone call with Brad Raffensperger and the subsequent consequences that occurred that the Georgia election process became a focus on my radar. From that time on, not only was I engaged in the election battle with Democrats in Washington D.C., but I was also keeping a close pulse on what was happening in Georgia. The Democrats continued to berate Georgia's election laws and portray them as "good old boy" politics. They made claims our election processes were skewed in the direction of benefiting Republicans. Nothing could have been further from the truth. They also continued to make a claim that our election laws were designed for suppression of minority voters. Again, the assertion was false.

It is extremely troubling to me the lengths to which some within the Democratic Party will go to push a narrative that does not exist. Don't get me wrong, I am fully aware that unscrupulous individuals inhabit the Republican Party as well. My intent is not to say, "All Democrats are bad, and Republicans are good." No. In fact, the preceding example illustrates a *Republican* Secretary of State who, either by back-room deals or by being outwitted, or by caving to fear and intimidation, made a horrible decision that endangered the most sacred voice that people have in American politics—their vote. There are plenty of places where stones could be thrown on either side of the aisle. Rather, my intent is simply to relay personal experiences in relation to the issue of election security and integrity. And to say that I am concerned . . . well, that's a major understatement! The Democrats were relentless in their attempts to frame a false narrative and then push it as factual, resulting in a major endeavor to federalize and seize national control of elections.

Let's take a closer look at the agreement between Brad Raffensperger and Stacey Abrams. The "Compromise Settlement Agreement and Release," was between the Democratic Party of Georgia, Inc., and Brad Raffensperger. Interestingly, one of the primary law firms representing the Democratic Party was Perkins Cole LLP. You might remember them; they have been in the news before. It appears this is the same firm that Hillary Clinton used to pay Fusion GPS and the DNC to produce the scandalous "Christopher Steele dossier." This is the report that ostensibly the FBI used to investigate the false and disproven Russian collusion charges that were levied against President

Trump. "The same dossier, which contained wild and unsub-
stantiated charges, was cited as purported evidence in four
successful FISA court applications to conduct surveillance on
Trump campaign adviser Carter Page."[2, 3] Obviously, the Georgia
Democrats spared no expense to hire the most experienced team
they could acquire. Likewise, it seems the Raffensperger legal
team was no match for the high-powered D.C. firm. They capit-
ulated as easy prey, being clearly outmaneuvered and outwitted.

The agreement, which was five pages in length, covered a
variety of issues, but the most significant, and the portion that
generated the most trepidation, dealt with signature matches.
Secretary of State Brad Raffensperger publicly claimed the
agreement strengthened signature verification, but in practical
application, countless Georgians opposed his assertion, and with
good reason. To summarize the agreed-upon change, if an elec-
tor's signature was questionable, the registrar or absentee ballot
clerk was required to review it with two others: another registrar, a deputy registrar, or an absentee ballot clerk. Upon review,
the absentee ballot in question could not be rejected without at
least two of the three officials agreeing that the signature did not
match any of the voter's signatures on file. Based upon requiring
two out of three persons to invalidate a signature, Raffensperger
maintained that he had created stronger standards.

What could possibly be wrong with his claim? Well, it appears
that although two out of three persons had to agree to reject a
signature and thus, the ballot, those officials making the decision were appointed by whichever party held the majority. In
other words, if the disputed ballot was in a Democratic area of
the state, then two of the three making the final decision would
be Democrats. The same would apply in a Republican area. But

obviously, the largest populations in Georgia include Atlanta and other large cities, all of which predominantly lean Democratic. We will never know how many ballots contained questionable signatures but were allowed to be counted by the "political majority," and those officials could be relatively certain that the ballot represented a vote that was favorable to their personal choice. Signature verification had ostensibly become a decision based upon the opinion of partisan officials, decided upon by the majority party. The concerns produced by this change were obvious and alarming. Indeed, the agreement was enormously problematic and produced great skepticism among millions of Georgia voters. And to make matters worse, it was virtually impossible for election personnel to meticulously authenticate the massive influx of absentee ballots that were received, nearly 1.4 million.

Another very disturbing aspect of the agreement involved how disputes would be resolved. Again, Raffensperger conceded the issue and approved that if any discrepancy were to arise, the sole and exclusive jurisdiction to resolve those disagreements would be the state courts located in Fulton County, Georgia. Again, Fulton County is the epicenter of Democratic politics in the state. For this partisan hotbed to have sole jurisdiction of disputed election matters could not possibly be considered wise or fair to any reasonable person. Rather, it essentially gave an advantage to Democrats. Instead, why not approve a contract based upon transparency and the absence of potential wrong-doing? Why not protect elections?

As mentioned, the agreement between Raffensperger and Abrams was approved on March 6, more than two weeks before the delegation had a phone call with him. The warnings we had given him proved to be accurate. Georgia's election was a disaster. Allegations of various types were abundant, from mass numbers of absentee ballots with little eligibility requirements, to apparent problems with voting machines, to chain-of-custody concerns, to voters being told they had already voted, and a host of other complications.

Not only did Secretary Brad Raffensperger deny the reality of any serious problems in the election, but he literally claimed that November 3 was "the most secure election in history." Meanwhile, his own deputy uncovered absentee ballot fraud that occurred from his own house. In a tweet that Gabriel (Gabe) Sterling posted on December 22, 2020, he said, "The woman I bought my house from over 2 years ago [is] trying to vote from it absentee 1/5. I've filed an official challenge to stop her from casting an apparently illegal vote." Fox 5 Atlanta wrote an article about this, describing how the woman voted in the presidential election by requesting an absentee ballot using the elected official's home address and then requesting an absentee ballot for the Senate runoffs in Georgia.[4] On that same day, Sterling said, "The Fulton Elections Board has acted and stated that my challenge to the qualifications of the woman—attempting to vote from the house I purchased from her 2 years ago meets probable cause." Not surprisingly, he experienced some backlash from left-wing individuals following his remarks, to which he defensively tweeted, "It's over 2 years. Over 2 full election cycles. She illegally voted in races here . . . she signed a sworn oath saying she lived in my home. I followed the process available to me under the law . . . I challenged her ability to cast a legal vote." Astonishing! This unbelievable scenario would be funny if it were not true. It is staggering to think that voter fraud was allegedly attempted from the home of a top-tier manager within the Secretary of State's office, yet Georgians were repeatedly told the election was the most secure in history.

By this point in time, two things were becoming abundantly clear to me. One, as the ranking member of the Subcommittee on Government Operations of the Oversight Committee, I needed to request a personal testimony from Secretary Raffensperger to the Republican members of our committee and have him explain the fiasco that had occurred in Georgia's election. Second, having become the point man from the Georgia delegation on the issue, I made the decision to challenge my state's certified electoral votes on January 6. That decision was met with no objection from my colleagues.

To petition his testimony, an official request had to be made to the Secretary of State. On December 15, 2020, a united number of 15 Republican committee members signed a letter to Secretary Brad Raffensperger requesting his appearance at a member-level briefing. The purpose of the briefing was clear: to have him answer questions regarding the multiple issues that had emerged from Georgia's November general election, and to ensure optimum election security for the two upcoming Senate runoff elections in January. To my great amazement, Raffensperger agreed to appear "virtually" before the Republican members of the government operations subcommittee.

Covid had provided Democrats an excuse to demand changes regarding election processes. That, combined with some horrible unilateral decisions by Brad Raffensperger, created the perfect storm over Georgia. Current election laws were ignored, and the

Secretary of State, rather than exercising discernment as to the sinister strategies at work, literally played into their hands and did the Left's dirty work for them, both by signing an agreement with Stacey Abrams' cronies and then by defending his actions before the media. Compared to 2018, mail-in voting increased by more than 500 percent in 2020. Correspondingly, the number of rejected absentee ballots dropped to 0.34 percent in the general election in 2020, from 3.46 percent in 2018.[5] In 2016, the rejection rate had been 2.9 percent.[6] Why was there such a significant decrease in the rejection rate? We needed answers.

As mentioned earlier, the agreement between Raffensperger and Democratic organizations also addressed the signature verification procedures. Increasing the number of people required to reject a signature made the undertaking more difficult to achieve. Further, before the Georgia Senate Judiciary Committee, a multitude of testimonies had been given accusing irregularities with chain of custody, counting of ballots, election observers not given access to do their jobs, and a host of other problems. Again, these serious concerns demanded answers, as did the video that apparently showed ballots being counted for hours after workers had been sent home in Fulton County.

At 11:00 a.m., on December 29, 2020, the member briefing took place. I honestly cannot say that we accomplished our goal. Although Raffensperger was present, his attorney and general counsel, Ryan Germany, did most of the talking for the secretary, and they were very illusive and lawyer-esque in providing answers. I was able, however, to ask two specific questions to Mr. Raffensperger, and to this day, his answer rings in my ear. The gist of my questions were:

Secretary Raffensperger, you made the unilateral decision
to send nearly seven million absentee ballot applications,
unsolicited, to every Georgia voter—despite knowing full well
that the voter rolls are not accurate. As a result, you have
opened the whole system to potential fraud. There have been
countless cases of households receiving multiple applications
for people who have not lived there in years, if ever. You were
warned beforehand this was a bad idea, but you persisted
anyway. To the best of my knowledge, you have not admitted
that this was a colossal mistake. Yet, you are now calling for an
end to "no excuse" absentee voting by mail. Sir, why did you
agree to flood the state with absentee ballot requests? And why
have you now changed your mind?

I don't vividly recall his answer to the second question, but his reply to the first startled me. Very simply and directly, he essentially said, "We feared a lawsuit from Stacey Abrams would be forthcoming if we did not send the absentee ballot applications to the entire voter file." Mr. Germany immediately chimed in to deflect what had just been stated. It was too late, the Secretary of State's answer had been straightforward, despite it not being an answer the general counsel wanted to hear. But the beans had been spilled. Raffensperger feared Stacey Abrams would file a lawsuit, so he caved to her demands to appease the threat!

It shouldn't be "breaking news," but the Secretary of State's office in Georgia gets sued on a regular basis. So why was he afraid of a Stacey Abrams lawsuit? Frankly, only Raffensperger and his team can answer that question, but the greater question is, "What is more important, defending against a lawsuit or defending a secure election for the people?" In my opinion, the moment he caved to her demands, the security of Georgia's election perished. When all is said and done, election integrity can only exist if people of integrity oversee the process. It does not matter if potential threats are involved or additional expense to the state might be extracted. When it comes to elections, the ultimate issue is, was the voice of the people accurately heard and reported? No other query matters. There is no other process that must be protected like elections, and no excuses for not doing so should be accepted. For those who have been entrusted to oversee the will of the people's vote, if they fail at that task, none of their other accomplishments matter. If they fail at securing elections, they have flunked their responsibility. Integrity matters, at every level.

7

Challenging Georgia's Certified Election

A false balance is an abomination to the Lord, but a just weight is his delight.

—PROVERBS 11:1

Integrity is keeping a commitment even after circumstances have changed.

—DAVID JEREMIAH

D URING THE 2020 ELECTION cycle, I became increasingly convinced that Georgia's election certification needed to be challenged in Washington, D.C., due to an abundance of abnormalities and unanswered questions. Allegations and testimonies were almost ceaseless regarding problems in the election, and it appeared as though the Secretary of State, Brad Raffensperger, was doing little to nothing to address the concerns. So numerous were the allegations that a special committee, known as the Election Law Study Subcommittee, which was a subcommittee of the Standing Judiciary Committee, was established by the Georgia state Senate to investigate the election. They were assigned the task of taking a deep dive into the election, under the leadership of Chairman William Ligon.

Their work resulted in a 15-page report of shocking and disparaging information. Among the findings, they concluded, "the November 3, 2020, election was chaotic, and the results cannot be trusted."[1] They cited multiple failures regarding enforcement of, or adherence to, state election laws, lack of transparency in signature verification, vote-counting concerns, and individual observers not having access to monitor the various processes involved. They also found ballots that were not secure, numerous procedures not followed, chain of custody failures, "outside" money that had been used to influence the election process, and an issue that went viral on the mainstream media—ballots seemingly being counted intentionally at State Farm Arena after observers had been dismissed and sent home.[2] They concluded, "The oral testimonies of witnesses on December 3, 2020, and subsequently, the written testimonies submitted by many others, provide ample evidence that the 2020 Georgia General Election was so compromised by systemic irregularities and voter fraud that it should not be certified."[3] It was this report that solidified my decision to challenge the results on January 6, as a U.S. Representative from Georgia.

Of course, little did I know that January 6 would soon be remembered as a day of "insurrection," as the U.S. Capitol Building would be overwhelmed by a mob of protestors and likely others who were involved as influencers to lure the crowd inside. To my knowledge, no one was ever charged with "insurrection" despite the term being used continuously by the

Democrats and legacy media. What took place that day was certainly wrong, but an insurrection? Hardly.

Nonetheless, although my home state was undoubtedly the case I was most familiar with, Georgia was not the only one reporting significant concerns with the election. Arizona, Pennsylvania, Wisconsin, Michigan, Nevada, and others had also experienced problems. As a result, several of my colleagues were planning to do the same as I: they would challenge the election results from their respective states. As one would expect, leading up to the challenge we spoke several times, primarily wondering about the process involved and what to expect when we offered an objection. None of us had answers, only speculation. Eventually, someone suggested that we should request a meeting with the White House to obtain clarity and to get answers. A meeting was arranged.

Not surprisingly, the media tried to portray our meetings as a behind-the-scenes attempt to strategize ways to overturn the election.[4] Nothing could be further from the truth. We simply wanted to know how the process involving an election challenge would take place. We were seeking information. That said, the meeting that drew the most attention took place on December 21. Again, it was portrayed as a meeting to strategize a pathway to overturn the election. I certainly can't speak for everyone, but that was not my intent, nor was it on the minds of the others in attendance, so far as I was aware. We were seeking information as to what our role would be as objectors to our states' certification. Sure, we believed there were problems with the election, serious problems. But to paint a picture of us trying to connive a way to illegally reverse the outcome is preposterous. The legal process to challenge a certification was already well established and had been utilized many times throughout the nation's history, and most recently, by Democrats. We simply wanted to know how the process would work and what would be expected from us.

Eleven members of Congress met with President Trump that day, as well as intermittent meetings with individuals such as Chief of Staff Mark Meadows, Rudy Giuliani, and Vice President Mike Pence. By this late date on the calendar, a tremendous amount of media attention was being directed toward the "election fraud" allegations, reportedly, they said, without supporting evidence to substantiate the claims. It seemed obvious to me that there was an extensive number of authentic issues and unanswered irregularities regarding the election, enough to at least compel us to slow down as a nation and make sure that the various state certifications were accurate. But the voices within the mainstream media were successful in leading the narrative, and thereby they augmented intense pressure to certify the results and move forward with a new administration.

Under these conditions, as January 6 drew closer, so swelled the weight upon each of us who were going to challenge the outcome. I don't recall a great deal of interaction by members of Congress that day at the White House; we mostly listened. But it wasn't until after lunch that most of us finally received, in the simplest of terms, an explanation regarding what to expect on the House Floor on January 6. As we sat in the Cabinet Room, the door opened, and Vice President Pence entered the room. Since he would be the one presiding over the electoral count, several in the room began asking him how the process to challenge the election would unfold and specifically, what our role would be. In his typical fashion of unpretentious plainness and straightforwardness, he simply said:

Well, when the name of your state is called about certifying
the results, you will stand and oppose the certification. Then
I will ask if a Senator is present who supports your challenge.
If no Senator voices agreement with your position, then the
state's certification will be accepted without further discussion.
On the other hand, if a Senator voices agreement with your
objection, then we will have two hours for you to make your
case, following which, we will vote to decide whether Congress
will accept or reject the certification.

That made perfect sense and provided us a track of expectation. For myself, after hearing the vice president's comments, I felt as though we had been overthinking the process. It was not nearly as complicated as we had imagined. I know there was a lot of attention placed on the vice president's role as the presiding officer of the electoral count, but in all honesty, that was neither my concern nor focus. My role was to challenge Georgia's certification and to compellingly present the reasons for my objection. I was content to assume others would determine the vice president's roles and responsibilities.

Of course, the adverse events of January 6 totally overshadowed the election challenge that would eventually take place on the House Floor. As I sat behind my office desk that morning, I recall hearing some noise outside the window, but I never gave it much attention. There are frequent protests in Washington, and I had become rather numb to the voices that frequently can be heard from one group or another, as they protested or supported a particular cause. No doubt, the First Amendment is alive and well in Washington, D.C., so the noise that could be faintly heard from my window that day was nothing new to me, and it certainly did not rise to any level of concern. As a result, I was clueless as to the events taking place outside the Capitol that day. In fact, although an invitation had been received days before, I had not seen it and was not even aware (until that day) that President Trump was having a rally in D.C. that morning. My staff knew my attention was absorbed in the challenge, so they didn't bother to inform me about the rally or the invitation to attend. My thoughts were absorbed with equipping myself for two hours that would be afforded to explain my "case" regarding the reasons why Georgia's electoral certification should be denied until a more thorough investigation could establish the accuracy of the count. Thus, in my office, I persisted in my own sort of "lockdown," in deep concentration and study. Georgia Senator Kelly Loeffler had agreed to support my challenge. So the upcoming presentation had to be precise, factual, and effectively articulated.

It was about 1:00 p.m. when I heard yelling in the hallway of my fourth floor Cannon Office Building. It was the U.S. Capitol Police. They were demanding the offices be evacuated. Again, knowing that I would soon need to be on the House Floor, I initially paid little attention to their demands and continued my last-minute preparation. Probably 20 minutes later, they were literally pounding on my office door, demanding that I follow them immediately. So I grabbed my computer, notes, and suit jacket, and followed them down the hallway while asking, "What's going on?" They informed me that a large crowd had gathered outside the Capitol, and they were responsible for the safety of congressional members. Again, I gave little thought as to the seriousness of the situation. I told them that I needed to immediately go to the House Floor to present my case but was outright denied the ability to leave their security. Instead, they lead me to their office in the basement of the Longworth House Office Building, where I stayed for about 30 minutes. Then, along with several others, I was lead via obscure passageways, to the Rayburn House Office Building. It was there, in the Oversight Committee Room area, that I was joined with others on my staff, along with freshman Congressman Andrew Clyde and his staff, also from Georgia.

It was not until then, when the TV was turned on, that we saw the crowds gathered and the potential seriousness of the situation. But even then, never did I feel threatened or unsafe on that day. In fact, I recall having an authentic sense of inner peace the entire time. I won't go into all the events that unfolded that day, as I am sure you have your own recollection. But I do applaud the decision for Congress to reconvene once the crowd was under control and the concerns about safety were banished. That was a good choice.

There was an overall sense of satisfaction and pride as Congress was gaveled into session that evening. The proceedings, having been delayed for several hours, were once again on the move. For such a time as this, we needed someone in the Chair who could appropriately lead us back into session, following a day filled with such turbulence. With calm sureness, Vice President Pence did a fine job in that regard. As he started calling roll through the various states for their electoral count, he finally called upon Georgia. As promised, I stood and objected to the certification numbers. I waited for what seemed to be an eternity for a response from Senator Loeffler, but she remained quiet. My heart began to pound. Why was she not speaking? Apparently shaken by the events of the day, she refused to challenge the certification from our state. The vice president said something to the effect of, "Hearing no favorable support for your objection from a Senator, the certification results from Georgia are accepted." I was so disappointed. After so much time, effort, and preparation, our challenge to the election indiscretions in Georgia had ended immediately and abruptly. I was speechless. Certainly, I can understand being rattled by the events of January 6, but those events did not change the fact that Georgia had had authentic failings within the election, and there were many questions that needed to be answered. To me, nothing had changed simply because of the unruly crowd. Our challenge should have gone forward. But it was now over, and the frustration I felt inside was enormous. As America would soon witness, the upcoming Senate runoff in Georgia brought forth victories for two extremely left-wing Democratic candidates. It seemed so surreal. How could a "red" state like Georgia elect two senators who were so Left-leaning? The Republican voters of Georgia were furious.

Following that Senate runoff, Georgia Secretary of State Brad Raffensperger became the recipient of much scrutiny. The state GOP was infuriated that he had ostensibly compromised the election by making an ill-advised agreement with Democrats, which potentially opened the door for unchecked fraudulent activity. The accusations against him skyrocketed. Everything about the election came into question, from the debacle created by absentee ballot requests being sent to the entire voter registration file, to unmonitored drop-off boxes, to lack of authentic signature verification, to apparent mischief in Fulton County, and a host of other issues—he was in the hot seat. The denunciation of his performance was so intense that on June 5 at the state

GOP convention, Raffensperger was censured by the party for "dereliction of his Constitutional duty."[5] Although the thought had never previously crossed my mind, it was during this general time frame that someone (I don't recall who) encouraged me to consider running against Raffensperger for the position of Secretary of State. The suggestion was like a dash of cold water in my face, it got my attention. That evening, I floated the idea by my wife, and astonishingly to me, she perked up to the idea. Following some discussion between us, we concluded that the idea was serious enough that we needed to pray about it, right then. So we joined hands and hearts, and knelt in front of our living room couch, asking God for wisdom. To be sure, not all our times of prayer are like this occasion, but it was not long before we concluded the prayer, and looking at one another, we both felt strongly that we should step into the race. The certainty we sensed at that moment was so strong that my wife said to me, "Jody, I think you are more equipped to be Secretary of State than you are to be a member of Congress!" Trying to keep my mouth from twitching, I responded something to the effect of, "Well, thanks for the affirmation, Hon, but I sure wish you would have told me that eight years ago. It would have saved us a lot of headaches!" Nonetheless, we were sensing a "green light" to pursue a new position, but we needed additional confirmation. Upon further discussion, we determined three or four factors that needed to happen for us to confidently move forward. Unquestionably, the biggest "fleece" we agreed upon would be the support and endorsement of President Trump.

To the best of my memory, it was the next day when Mark Meadows unexpectedly called me. Mark was a dear friend. He and Deb had taken Dee Dee and me under their wings eight years earlier. I had been an original member of the House Freedom Caucus, and prior to him becoming chief of staff at the White House, Mark had not only been an outstanding leader in Congress, but he also had served as chairman of the House Freedom Caucus, having followed the equally tremendous leadership of our first chairman, Jim Jordan. Although I always felt particularly close with Mark, we didn't talk frequently, only when something specific was on our minds. So after some brief and customary words that accompany most conversations, he got straight to the point. "Jody," he said, "what are we going to do about Georgia's Secretary of State? Somebody needs to challenge Raffensperger!" I was taken aback. It probably required only a few seconds, but it seemed to take minutes to gain my composure. I'm sure my response was given in a somewhat nervous but precise fashion. "Mark," I said, "Dee Dee and I have sincerely prayed about this, and we believe that I need to run for that position. I've been on the cutting edge of this issue for a long time, and within the Georgia delegation, I've been the most vocal about election matters. . . . I believe I need to challenge Mr. Raffensperger." After a brief silence that seemed to be both appropriate and thoughtful, he replied. "Wow. That's great. But are you sure? We would hate to lose you in Congress." After several additional minutes of dialogue, I presented to him one of the conditions we had determined would be necessary for us to pursue the race. "Mark, do you think President Trump would be willing to endorse me?" Although I had been in several meetings with the president, I did not have a close relationship with him at the time. Without much hesitation, he replied, "I think he will. Let me ask him." Before we ended the phone call, he once again stated, "I will talk with the president and get back to you." The conversation soon ended. And with a sense of inner peace, we rested.

Within a couple of days, Mark informed me of the president's willingness to endorse my candidacy for Secretary of State, but that he wanted to speak with me in person first. In relatively short order, arrangements were made for us to talk. When I received his call from the White House, I was deeply moved by the president's words of support and affirmation. He began the conversation by asking, "Are you sure this is something you want to do?" He continued, "You've got a great position in Congress, and you are doing a wonderful job . . . we would hate to lose you there, but I will support you if you choose to leave." I thanked him and then assured him of my intentions to challenge Raffensperger. Amusingly, he then said, "Well, if you are going to leave Congress, would you be willing to run for governor? I think you would make a great governor!" If a smile and chuckle could be transferred across the phone, he would have seen my delighted grin. But I simply communicated that my desire was to correct the election problems that Georgia had experienced, and the only way to accomplish that was through the Secretary of State's office. He agreed and willingly pledged his support.

From that time forward, we stayed in contact, talking at least once every couple of weeks and occasionally, a few times a week. I honestly wish everyone had the opportunity to know President Trump in the way I came to know him. To me, he was an extremely enjoyable person. Like all of us, he has flaws, but he certainly is not the monster that some have tried to construct. He is very funny and quick-witted, exceptionally smart, very personal, and deeply passionate about America. On the other hand, when it's time for business, he is all business. He is a man of action and does not tolerate complacency. That's precisely why he was able to get so much accomplished during his time in the White House. He loves moving the needle forward and has an uncanny ability to do so. As I look back on those days, I am filled with a sense of marvel. It is unreal that I had the opportunity to develop such a meaningful relationship with the president of the United States, Donald Trump. I will forever cherish the conversations and times we spent together and am enormously grateful for his personal support, and for the kindness he extended to me and Dee Dee. Frankly, he quickly developed a fondness for Dee Dee, as she always had the right words to say to him. She spoke from the heart and always made him smile. On more than one occasion, he told me that she is the one who ought to run. "She is a much better candidate than you are," he would say. And although he made those comments with a humorous grin, he was sincerely communicating his heartfelt affection for her unpretentious kindness and sweet disposition.

Nonetheless, our campaign for Secretary of State was underway. Many thought the defeat of Brad Raffensperger would be a cakewalk. But from the beginning, I and our campaign team knew this would be an uphill battle even though Raffensperger was very unpopular. After all, taking down an incumbent official in Georgia is hard, but defeating one in your own party is even more difficult. We inquired of state political historians, and they could not recall this ever being done. Still, I believed this was the right thing to do, given the secretary's unforced errors throughout the 2020 election cycle. I felt Georgians should have another choice for the office, so I stepped up to the plate and was all in. The only caveat was that upon entering the race, I would not let my campaign for statewide office get in the way of my official duties as a Congressman. In other words, I would not miss votes for the campaign, and I would continue to serve my constituents to the best of my ability throughout the race for statewide office. Thus, a 63-week campaign consisted of me being in Georgia for 35 weeks and being in Washington, D.C., for 28 weeks.

Our ground game was strong. The staff we had assembled was lean and mean, consisting of a campaign manager, a body guy, and field rep. These are generic titles that virtually all state or federal campaigns have, and the work they did was extraordinary. They helped us produce a robust internship program of 12 members, all of whom seemed to possess poise and a work ethic far beyond their age. Thus, our 15-person core team and the 2,512-volunteer army they recruited executed 602,000 dials and 24,684 door knocks. When I was in Georgia, we were constantly on the road visiting with people across the entire state. Our campaign team and I covered 257 events in 103 counties during the campaign, which lasted a little over a year.

The press strategy for the campaign was simple. From my time serving in Congress, I had already garnered most of the support from viewers of conservative news outlets. So we continued going on those shows as time and opportunity allowed. On the other hand, we largely avoided liberal media outlets. Very few people watching those programs would ever vote for me, and besides, those reporters simply wanted to portray a 60-year-old grandpa, devoted husband, and conservative Christian congressman as an enemy of democracy. I had experienced enough of their deceitful methods in Washington and saw no point in wasting my time trying to mentally navigate through their devious questions, which were designed to make me say something that could be used against me. Nonetheless, they often showed up at places where I was speaking, and we would almost always accommodate their request for a brief interview. We hosted numerous events, including many from a strategically launched three-day, 12-city "fly around" tour. Every region of the state welcomed us as we held a series of rallies to galvanize our base throughout. In addition, the fly-around provided an opportunity for press conferences with as many news agencies as wanted to attend, including some we wished had not attended. Everyone from the *New York Times* to the most right-leaning news organizations joined in the experience as I did interviews with dozens of state and national outlets during that three-day period.

Some critics argued that my time being divided between congressional responsibilities and campaign efforts would prevent me from successfully raising enough money for a winning operation. They were wrong. I raised nearly $2.5 million, while all my competitors combined, including the incumbent, raised only $1.7 million. This does not include the incumbent's loan to himself of approximately $875,000.

The message of the campaign was clear. I was running to restore election integrity to Georgia's office of Secretary of State. As stated previously, I believed the mass mailing of absentee ballot requests to the entire state was irresponsible and it opened the door for fraud. Further, I wanted to improve the General Assembly's Bill, SB 202, by eliminating drop boxes and outside funding in elections. As stated, I was deeply honored to have the endorsement of President Trump, but I did not enter the race because of him, nor did he ever ask me to run. I was in this race for three primary reasons. First, because I had developed an awareness and grave concerns about election integrity following the Democrats' attempt to introduce federal legislation to nationalize elections. Their attempt had come through one of my committees, Oversight, nearly three years before. Election integrity had been on my radar ever since. I had fought against the passage of their legislation and strongly supported the right of states to determine the time, place, and manner of elections, as the U.S. Constitution mandates. Second, the widespread issues that overwhelmed Georgia demanded someone to take a stand, and it seemed only natural for that "someone" to be me. Finally, we strongly believed the Lord had given us a "green light" to proceed.

Our paid voter contact plan started early in the campaign before the airwaves were cluttered. We aired almost 6,000 television commercials statewide, in every market. We did this during two different "flights" in two six-week time spans. The buy was cable TV, as traditional down-ballot media buys typically are. We also sustained a moderate to heavy radio presence on 13 to 15 conservative talk radio programs across the state. In all, the campaign was on radio for seven weeks, two flights complementing the TV buy, and a third flight for the last three weeks of the campaign.

In addition, the campaign launched nearly 250,000 text messages and over 36,000 robocalls promoting my candidacy and letting people know when I would be in a geographic area for an event. There were also 726,000 text messages and robocalls sent to voters to shore up support, and 200,000 get-out-the-vote robocalls and text messages. When combined with over 625,000 doors and dials, this made for a robust, well-rounded voter-contact plan.

The polling we did, and the decisions to spend or not spend money, were deliberate and intentional. The firm used by our campaign consultants was the same one they had used for over eight years. They had never gotten a primary wrong, and frankly, I don't believe they got this one wrong either. But what we could never have seen coming was a ground shifting that took place extremely late in the election cycle.

In late December, we saw an outside chance for me to win without a runoff. This was coming off the heels of a media buy, and we knew things would tighten up once we hit election year. But at that time, things looked and felt good. In February, it appeared that our campaign was headed for a runoff, something that we had frankly expected from the beginning, although many people did not understand why Raffensperger could not be defeated outright. Going into early voting, around the second week of tracking, we noticed Raffensperger's "attack ads" were starting to resonate with potential voters, and a portion of my supporters were beginning to move into the "undecided" category. We quickly commenced research to identify the specific part of the electorate that needed to be addressed and what would resonate with them. As a result, we initiated a voter-contact plan to correct the issue, and the tracking poll was corrected in short order, and we moved on.

Midway through early voting, we were shocked to see the turnout was astronomical. We, along with many in the political world, wanted to know who these new people were. Where were these people coming from? As it turned out, many were traditional Republicans, many were new to the process, and a significant number were Democrats. Unbelievably, there was a well-organized plan for Democrats to "cross over" and vote for Raffensperger. After all, he had done their bidding for them, and they did not want him to leave office. To the best of our ability, we polled this universe of people, and our campaign was still 10 points up. While we were at it, we also polled the people who had not yet voted but who were projected to vote on Election Day. Those margins were a little tighter but nothing for us to worry about. This made sense because Brad had started his contrast ads very late. Everything in our data said that my floor, or the worst I could expect, was about 41 percent, and the ceiling was 48 percent for the primary election. My campaign team thought we would end up between 44 and 46 percent. With four people in the race, this would certainly put us in a runoff with Raffensperger, and we were OK with that scenario. Thus, we decided to deploy the rest of our primary cash into another round of voter contact to make sure this was the case and to prepare for a runoff. The campaign had no more uncommitted primary cash available on Election Day. At that time, whatever money people saw in the bank was runoff and general election money that was returned to donors.

When all was over, the voter turnout broke every model. The incumbent and outside groups doubled down and created a pathway for him to be re-elected. In our estimations, the maximum turnout would be approximately 850,000. Never could we have imagined seeing nearly 1.2 million Georgians vote in the Secretary of State's race. Further, Brad invested a large sum of his own resources late in the race. His attacks on digital outlets were vicious against me, while promoting himself as the warrior of election integrity, which was pathetic. But combining the dramatic increase in voter turnout consisting of nontraditional Republican primary voters as well as new voters and Democratic voters, and the incumbent had a heyday. Raffensperger won without a runoff, getting 52 percent of the vote to my 34 percent.

How could this be? The statistical worst-case scenario for me was 41 percent, which still would have forced a runoff. Literally, it felt like the numbers had been inverted. The incumbent and outside groups spent over $2 million against me on the last three weeks of the campaign. No doubt, that is a difficult hurdle to overcome. Nonetheless, people throughout the state were stunned by the outcome. Had there been shenanigans behind the scenes? We will never know. Efforts to investigate or simply compare the printed votes with the electronic results were denied. Why? Here again, transparency is essential if voter confidence is to be realized. Common sense should rule the day—if there is nothing to hide, then be transparent.

To be clear, I am not necessarily making an accusation of wrongdoing. I have accepted defeat, and I have moved on with my life. But I do have many questions about the election that remain unanswered. Indeed, something smells fishy. For example, one of the most conservative congressional districts in the nation is GA-14, home of Marjorie Taylor Greene. It is arguably the "reddest" and most pro-Trump district in Georgia. Yet, most GA-14 counties voted for the incumbent Raffensperger, despite both Marjorie Taylor Greene and Trump supporting me. Keep in mind, Raffensperger was very unpopular, and that fact was amplified in GA-14. For all practical purposes, he could not even host meetings in that region of the state without being booed off the stage. This is but one example of hundreds. There are many questions that beg for answers. Unpretentious transparency would be a great place to begin.

We will never know all the details of my race, and that is the problem! We never acquired any polling that indicated such an outcome, not even remotely. And national pollsters said the same. About two weeks prior to the election, in a Freedom Caucus meeting in Washington, D.C., a pollster of national acclaim was at our meeting to discuss various races across the country. During that discussion, someone asked him about Georgia's Secretary of State race. I'm sure the question arose because of me. Without hesitation, he chuckled and said with great confidence, "Brad Raffensperger has *zero* chance of winning. He is toast!" I will not mention the name of the pollster due to his high regard, but obviously his research said the same as ours, and he was as shocked by the results as we were.

Why do I mention all of this? I'm certainly not bitter, nor am I trying to win sympathy or make excuses for losing by interjecting suspicion into the outcome. But when all is said and done, elections are not simply about who wins or loses; the ultimate issue is integrity, whether it was a fair and honest vote. And when it comes to integrity, transparency is essential. Elections must be protected, and the citizens must be confident that the process is fair and accurate. Never give up on this ideal. America depends on it!

8

Why Election Integrity Matters

Moreover, look for able men from all the people, men who fear God, who are trustworthy and hate a bribe, and place such men over the people as chiefs of thousands, of hundreds, of fifties, and of tens.

—EXODUS 18:21

A true leader has the confidence to stand alone, the courage to make tough decisions, and the compassion to listen to the needs of others. He does not set out to be a leader, but becomes one by the equality of the actions and the integrity of his intent.

—DOUGLAS MACARTHUR

IT IS INCUMBENT UPON every American to take seriously the privilege and duty of voting. I do not believe it can be emphasized enough, nor is it an exaggeration to assert that the health, well-being, and future of our republic depend upon the faithful and thoughtful votes of American citizens. Within the context

111

of our political structure, we understand that if unprincipled individuals are elected to office, then unprincipled laws and behavior will result. Everyone suffers when the representatives of the people, be they those serving as legislators, judges, or executives, operate with selfish motives or engage in corruption. In America, the greatest guard against such a travesty is the people's voice. Make no mistake, our political system functions properly only when the voice of the people is adequately and fairly expressed at the ballot box. It is there, in the secret place of an individual vote, that we have the opportunity, yes, the duty, to elect principled individuals to represent us. To say it another way, in a political system such as ours, it is impossible to maintain and sustain our republic, which is based upon maximum liberty and limited government, without honorable people representing the citizens and defending our political and unalienable foundation. And all citizens have a role to play in protecting our democracy and faithfully passing it to the next generation. At a time when the foundations of our country seem to be rotting away, never has it been more vital that the voice and will of citizens be heard. How could anyone possibly act as though elections do not matter?

It has been said that "eternal vigilance is the price of liberty." When we take time to ponder that statement, the truth of it is unmistakable. Deep down, we understand that politics tends to grab power and restrict freedom over the course of time. We also recognize that within the political structure that we have in America, "We the people" are the ones who ultimately determine our leaders and thus, the political culture under which we all live. From that context, "eternal vigilance" demands our continual inspection of those elected officials, and the obligation to hold them accountable. Only when this takes place can liberty be assured for the next generation of Americans. Indeed, we are the ones responsible to pass liberty, and for that to happen, we must ensure that fair elections are protected.

I realize that the following story can easily be taken out of context. My intent in sharing this is not to portray my agreement with the actions that these individuals took; in fact, I do not. The truth is, my initial discovery of this occurrence shocked me, as I'm sure it will you also. Nonetheless, the following story is real. It is part of our American history. And it is a clear reminder of how important it is that previous generations embraced the concept of fair elections and their outright refusal to accept anything less. There has been much written regarding the event I am about to summarize, including a book entitled *The Fighting Bunch* by Chris DeRose. I certainly encourage you to dive further into the topic if you choose. Known as the "Battle of Athens," it was the shortest and only successful armed uprising in America since the Revolutionary War. And although it was widely covered by national news at the time, this important conflict, which started and concluded on August 1, 1946, has largely been ignored and forgotten.

Located in the beautiful rolling hills between Chattanooga and Knoxville, Tennessee, Athens is the county seat of McMinn County. The backdrop of this story involves political corruption and the determination of citizens, primarily a group of veterans who had recently returned from World War II, who refused to stand by while an election was being stolen. After several years of fraudulent elections, many within the community decided they needed to remove their corrupt leaders. As a result, an extremely spirited race for local positions ensued. The reasons for community-wide disdain for the status quo were obvious. According to descriptions, scandalous activities and political malpractice had been rampant under the leadership of a state senator, Paul Cantrell, and the local sheriff, Pat Mansfield. And now in cooperation with another ringleader out of Memphis, Ed Crump, they were trying to steal another election. By any standard, the list of their scandalous behavior was reprehensible and was known throughout the entire region. For example, for large sums of money, the "ring" protected secret gatherings of gamblers and bootleggers. Frequently, they were known to arrest local citizens and tourists for concocted charges like drunkenness and then requiring them to pay fines for release. In fact, there were even occasions of commercial buses traveling through the county being stopped and sleepy passengers being dragged off the bus and arrested for drunkenness. A good weekend for the sleazy politicians involved as many as 115 people being arrested, and each being forced to pay a significant sum of money to avoid arrest or some other legal harm to their reputation.[1] Through a mass litany of corrupt goings-on, they had developed a huge money-making machine in the county and were lining their own pockets with enormous amounts of cash. The only way to conceal their criminal behavior and to ensure continued cash flow was to protect their election.

Unfortunately, the scandals and exploitation had become a pattern year after year. And by creating a wall of protection around themselves, the politicians had become more emboldened and brash with time. On the other side, citizens developed a bigger sense of hopelessness to replace the crooked elites. Although local citizens had repeatedly tried to report the corruption to state and other legal authorities, every attempt had been met with obstruction, stonewalling, and a refusal to address the problems. At a point of total frustration and exacerbation, a group of citizens took matters into their own hands.

The oath of enlistment for military personnel says, "I do solemnly swear (or affirm) that I will support and defend the Constitution of the United States against all enemies, foreign and domestic; that I will bear true faith and allegiance to the same . . . ." It is the "foreign *and domestic*" portion of the oath that rose to prominence on this occasion. This group of soldiers had been willing to give their lives for freedom. Indeed, they were part of the "Greatest Generation," and their patriotic blood was authentic. Upon returning from the European and Pacific theaters in 1945 and 1946, it is no surprise that many of them were shocked to discover the depth of corruption and undemocratic processes that had taken over various parts of our country. Athens, Tennessee, was one such place. Both the city and county had become shrouded by the very corruption that the soldiers had been actively fighting against during World War II. For those who returned to Athens, the situation was more than they could endure. Not only had the economic situation become stagnant, and the educational system underperforming, but it was also the political vice that was totally unacceptable.

Inside the local jailhouse, Sheriff Pat Mansfield and state Senator Paul Cantrell were in the process of literally stealing the election. They had locked themselves inside the building and were "counting" the ballots. This closed-door scheme had become the standard method of determining election results in recent years. This time, however, a small band of veterans gathered outside the building and demanded changes from the current devious process and assurances for honest and transparent election results. The crooked politicians refused to comply. Inside their shelter, as had been the case time and again in recent years, they were confident of another victory as they "counted" the ballots. But on this occasion, things were about to change.

Following several unanswered demands by a growing number of veterans, the freedom-loving soldiers developed a plan. They broke into the local National Guard Armory facility, seized weapons and munitions, and immediately returned to the jail, demanding transparency with the election count. By this time, hundreds of veterans were on the scene as word of mouth was spreading like a wildfire. They repeatedly vocalized warnings and demands, but the deputies refused to oblige the requests. Using the skills and training they had acquired while in the military service, the veterans opened fire. The battle that followed lasted for several hours and included the overturning of several police cars and rioting. On the inside of the building, the political thugs refused to yield, that is, until the veterans dynamited the front of the jailhouse. The veterans meant business, and the explosion of the front door erased any false impressions that those on the inside might have had to the contrary. Amazingly, no one died on August 1, 1946. But even more important, neither did democracy die!

The corrupt political machine was broken that day, and fair elections were restored. Of the 12 ballot boxes that were taken, six were disposed of due to obvious tampering by Cantrell and his cronies. The other ballots showed an overwhelming victory for the candidates who ran against the corrupt leaders.[2] It is interesting to me that one of the most pertinent comments relating to the Battle of Athens came from none other than former First Lady Eleanor Roosevelt. She stated, "If a political machine does not allow the people free expression, then freedom-loving people lose their faith in the machinery under which their government functions." She went on to explain that if governments fail to recognize and guarantee the will of the people, "their days are numbered."[3]

No doubt, beyond First Lady Roosevelt, many other people also had opinions as to what took place that day, some positive and some negative. Again, my interest and focus are not to defend or negate the actions of those veterans; others have and will continue to make those assessments. However, regardless of your opinion of their actions, it is the motive behind their actions that should be highlighted. They possessed an absolute commitment to election integrity. That was their impetus. Secure elections should be viewed as something sacred. They represent the primary voice and method that "We the people" possess to determine both the leaders and the policies under which we live as Americans. Never should anything else be tolerated. As I said on the campaign trail over and over, there should be only "one legal ballot cast, and one legal ballot counted" for each person going to the polls. When everything else is said and done, it should be that simple, regardless of political affiliation.

I suppose one could argue that the Battle of Athens affirms nothing other than a commitment by some World War II veterans in relation to election integrity. But the deeper question is whether other generations would have been as committed. In other words, has the importance of honest, protected elections constantly been significant in America? Well, the short answer is, yes. Obviously, the examples that could be cited might easily involve multiple volumes. But to give a mere sample of our historical commitment to undefiled elections, allow me to cite just a few. Let us begin with the words of a prominent physician, a revolutionary, an educator, a Founding Father, and a signer of the Declaration of Independence. Benjamin Rush, in 1786, wrote a treatise entitled, "Thoughts Upon the Mode of Education Proper in a Republic." In that essay, he affirmed, "every citizen of a republic . . . must watch for the state as if its liberties depended upon his vigilance alone."[4] What a powerful statement. By using the word "watch," he was referring to much more than a simplistic visual evaluation—to specific action. He was pointing toward citizens being involved in defending our liberties through voting and personal engagement. His statement drives to the heart of citizenship and moves the reader to conclude that he believed every citizen should carry the weight of liberty upon his or her individual shoulders, as though the entire well-being of our nation rested upon them alone. And it is interesting to note, his exposition was precisely directed toward education in America, not elections. But he saw a distinct connection between the two. Every voter should be an educated voter, one who is informed on both issues and candidates. He also could not visualize an educational system in our republic that did not include imparting to young citizens the responsibility that they must personally embrace liberty, defend it, and be fortified to pass it on. Of foremost importance, this happens through fair elections.

Further, because the "American Experiment" was unique to the world, elections were not something to be taken lightly. John Jay, the first chief justice of the U.S. Supreme Court, said, "The Americans are the first people whom Heaven has favored with an opportunity of deliberating upon and choosing the forms of government under which they should live."[5] Imagine, nowhere else in the world were people allowed to determine their leaders, only in America. Thus, the deep sense of sacred dependance to wisely choose government leaders was considered essential for the well-being of the nation, both for the present and for future generations.

Another example involves a personal favorite, President James A. Garfield. In a speech given on July 4, 1876, on the 100th anniversary of the Declaration of Independence, he said:

> *Now, more than ever, the people are responsible for the*
> *character of their Congress. If that body be ignorant, reckless,*
> *and corrupt, it is because the people tolerate ignorance,*
> *recklessness, and corruption. If it be intelligent, brave, and pure,*
> *it is because the people demand these high qualities to represent*
> *them in the national legislature . . . if the next Centennial does*
> *not find us a great nation . . . it will be because those [people]*
> *who represent the enterprise, the culture, and the morality of*
> *the nation do not aid in controlling the political forces.*

I honestly have no idea how many hundreds of times I have used this Garfield quote when speaking to various groups or individuals. To me, his mindset is as relevant today as when first spoken, maybe more so. Many people believe Washington, D.C., is broken and filled with self-seeking, power-hungry politicians. Well, the citizens elected them! Do you believe some of those politicians should be replaced? If so, the power to do so rests within the will and power of the electorate. Good or bad, the individuals who represent us, be it local, state, or federal, are but a reflection of the people who voted them into office.

Again, this is a major distinction between America and the rest of the world. The people of this country control their political destiny. "We the People" can determine our leaders, and if they ever prove to be worthy of replacement, we have the power and the responsibility to "fire" them.

Jonathan Mayhew (1720–1766) said as much. Mayhew was an influential Congregationalist minister as well as a distinguished lecturer at Harvard. It was his firm conviction that elected officials could disqualify themselves from serving, even after holding office. In 1765, while reflecting on King George III's tyrannical attitude as a leader and his despised Stamp Act, Mayhew said:

> *The king is as much bound by his oath not to infringe the legal rights of the people, as the people are bound to yield subjection to him. From whence it follows that as soon as the prince sets himself above the law, he loses the king in the tyrant. He does, to all intents and purposes, un-king himself.*[6]

In other words, for a king (politician) to rule in a manner that is not in the best interest of the people, Mayhew believed the "king" could disqualify himself from serving. That is a great thought, but more easily said than done. In America, however, our system goes beyond the theory of political right and wrong and gives citizens the tools and realistic ability to replace the "king," if needed, through elections.

And Noah Webster, known for his dictionary of the English language and often referred to as the "Father of American Scholarship and Education," had some insightful comments regarding elections and the responsibility of voters. He said:

. . . God commands you to choose for rulers, just men who
will rule in the fear of God. The preservation of a republican
government depends on the faithful discharge of this duty; if the
citizens neglect their duty and place unprincipled men in office,
the government will soon be corrupted; laws will be made, not
for the public good, so much as for selfish or local purposes;
corrupt or incompetent men will be appointed to execute the
laws; the public revenues will be squandered on unworthy men;
and the rights of the citizens will be violated or disregarded.[7]

This comment is so accurate for contemporary America, it is as
though Webster was giving a present-day analysis. Notice the
spiritual responsibility that he emphasized, "God commands
you . . . ." To him, voting was a sacred trust and responsibility,
not simply a matter of personal preference or party affiliation. It
required divine discernment on the part of the voter, resulting
in a deliberate selection for morally guided individuals. Why
would he link God and voting? The architects who shaped the
foundation of America had a supernatural understanding of the
indispensable requirements for sustaining freedom. To them,
the significance of elections was surpassed only by the importance of true moral character among those who were elected.
There was a clear connection. The only way for morally stout
individuals to lead our country was for them to be elected by
the people. Ultimately, everything rested upon the citizens to
select quality leaders. Thus, when the people went to the ballot box, they needed discernment regarding the most qualified.
This, according to Webster and others, required divine assistance. Both elements were essential—informed voters and morally sound leaders. Unless this combination were in balance,

the American experiment would not long endure. To preserve maximum liberty for individuals on the one side and limited government on the other, elections must hold a hallowed position both to the individual voter and the country.

And speaking of elections being attached to spiritual responsibility, Billy Graham once said, "If America is to survive, we must elect more God-centered men and women to public office—individuals who will seek divine guidance in the affairs of state."[8] Again, notice the importance of character; it simply cannot be overemphasized. To Graham, having "God-centered men and women" in public office was essential for the survival of our nation. Quite frankly, it is difficult to argue an opposing position. Without elected officials possessing moral character, just laws and impartial justice would be nothing but a dream. However, when leaders recognize their role, under God, to administer fundamental principles of liberty for all, then everyone benefits, and America will remain free, strong, and prosperous. But if corruption is permitted within leaders, it will eventually permeate to all levels of society. It is extremely difficult to ignore the reality that the further America has drifted away from morality and biblical principles, the more corrupt and feebler our country has become. Everything ultimately rises or falls upon leadership, and the question of leadership depends upon the people choosing individuals of supreme moral character. May we always know, elections are a sacred responsibility and should be regarded as such, by everyone who enters the private voting booth.

9

When Election Integrity Fails

The righteousness of the blameless keeps his way straight, but the wicked falls by his own wickedness.

—PROVERBS 11:5

If you have integrity, nothing else matters. If you don't have integrity, nothing else matters.

—ALAN K. SIMPSON

I T SEEMS LIKE A distant memory at this point, but before 2020, electoral fraud was a routinely discussed topic and deeply concerning to all Americans. While it's comforting to believe that the American electoral system has always been sacred, sacrosanct, and beyond reproach, there is a long and dark history of rogue actors and malicious party operatives who have attempted to subvert democracy by stealing the election. While some were uncovered before they could enact their nefarious plans, there have been many elections won under questionable conditions that were nevertheless permitted to stand.

The "Box 13" Scandal

The 1948 Texas Senate election saw former Governor Coke Stevenson and Democratic Congressman Lyndon B. Johnson face off for the Democratic nomination. Both candidates struggled through the tightly contested primary and faced a runoff election. The status of Texas at that time as a blue stronghold meant that the winner was a likely shoo-in for the general election. On the evening of the runoff, Stevenson held a slim lead over Johnson.

However, the tide dramatically turned in favor of Johnson when 202 additional votes were discovered in Precinct 13, hence the name "Box 13." These additional votes were in favor of Johnson, which ultimately allowed him to secure a narrow victory by just 87 votes. The suspicious nature of the late-discovered votes and their overwhelming support for Johnson raised immediate concerns of election fraud.

Accusations of ballot box stuffing and irregularities quickly surfaced. It was alleged that the 202 votes were fraudulent and had been added to the count after the polls had closed. Witnesses claimed that they saw election officials manipulating the ballot box, and there were reports of altered poll books and questionable signatures on some of the added ballots.[1]

The controversy led to a brutal legal battle. Stevenson contested the election results. He alleged fraud and sought a complete recount of the entire race. However, his efforts were ultimately unsuccessful. The court ruled in favor of Johnson, citing insufficient evidence to prove systematic fraud or manipulation that would overturn the election results. Lyndon B. Johnson was declared the winner, propelling him to the U.S. Senate and setting him on a path that eventually led to the presidency.

To be clear, the court case by no means exonerated Johnson. The court ruled in favor of him due to "insufficient evidence," not innocence. This race left Johnson with the reputation of a shrewd and cunning candidate who would stop at nothing to achieve victory. It also caused millions of Texans to question the integrity of their entire electoral system.

Not long after the election, Texas implemented a slew of electoral reforms to enhance transparency and ensure the accuracy of election results, including stricter regulations on ballot counting and the introduction of additional oversight measures.

The lesson from this incident is that regardless of whether there was foul play, a bipartisan group of legislators realized that the only way to ensure the integrity of the system was with absolute transparency. Therefore, in the face of doubt they did everything in their power to reform the system in the hope that it would restore faith and integrity.

If only Democrats had done the same in 2020. If they had worked with Republicans to reform and restore our elections, they could have restored faith to millions of people. Instead, they played politics and obstructed Republicans at every turn. They stymied even some of the most popular of election integrity laws. The legacy of that partisan cravenness still haunts our elections to this day.

Boss Tweed and Tammany Hall

In the late nineteenth century, boss politics and political machines had a profound influence on American elections. The rapid industrialization of America and the millions of immigrants who followed led to the creation of massive political organizations commonly known as "political machines."

These networks usually consisted of a handful of key individuals who maintained major positions of power through bribery, graft, corruption, and the ability to sway large groups of voters. Political machines existed as far back as the eighteenth century, but the economic growth following the reconstruction era permitted their reach and corruption to flourish like never before.

Arguably the most famous of these political machines was William Magear Tweed and the legendary corruption of the Democrats' Tammany Hall. Tweed, or "Boss Tweed," as he was commonly known, was a former New York congressman who became infamous for using various positions in the state government to reward supporters with government jobs and contracts. By controlling key positions, Tweed and his associates maintained a network of loyalists who owed their livelihoods to the political machine. This patronage system allowed them to exert significant influence over the electoral process, as employees were expected to deliver votes and campaign on behalf of Tammany Hall–endorsed candidates.

The financial graft of Tammany Hall has been well documented, but its critical role in voter intimidation and fraud is often overlooked. This involved manipulating voter registration lists, bribing election officials, and using violence to suppress opposition and deter voters. Through these coercive measures, Boss Tweed and his allies maintained a tight grip on the electoral process, ensuring the success of Tammany Hall–backed candidates. By 1870, every position on New York City's Common Council was filled with a Tweed Loyalist.

Tweed also exploited their political power to manipulate district boundaries and influence redistricting efforts. By strategically carving out districts, they could concentrate opposition voters in certain areas, diluting their political influence. This gerrymandering allowed Tammany Hall to consolidate power and control election outcomes at the district level.

Yet, none of this corruption would have been possible without a pliable and corrupt media apparatus. Boss Tweed and Tammany Hall exercised significant control over the media, ensuring favorable coverage and suppressing dissenting voices. Through bribes, threats, and other forms of coercion, Boss Tweed and his associates were able to gain significant influence over various newspapers and journalists. They ensured that these media outlets published favorable stories that portrayed Tweed and his political machine in a positive light while suppressing or distorting any negative information or criticism. This manipulation allowed Tweed to craft a carefully curated public image, presenting himself as a benefactor of the working class, while he was exploiting the city for personal gain and siphoning off millions of dollars in corrupt deals.

The media's collaboration with Boss Tweed not only shielded him from scrutiny but also helped him solidify his power and control over New York City. By controlling the narrative and suppressing dissenting voices, Tweed was able to maintain a tight grip on the political landscape and ensure his re-elections and appointments of loyal allies to various positions of power. The corrupt alliance between Boss Tweed and the media ultimately led to widespread public outrage once the truth of the corruption came to light, sparking a significant reform movement and eventually contributing to Tweed's downfall and imprisonment.

While Tweed controlled many publications, a few brave and intrepid journalists refused to appease Tweed and took a powerful stand. Thomas Nast, a cartoonist for *Harper's Weekly* used his platform to satirize and expose the rampant corruption within Tweed's political machine. His powerful and evocative illustrations depicted Tweed and his associates engaging in bribery, cronyism, and embezzlement, effectively bringing these issues to the public's attention, and creating a strong sense of public outrage.

In addition to Nast's incriminatory cartoons, a group of political reformers and concerned citizens known as the Committee of Seventy played a crucial role in bringing down Boss Tweed. This group was dedicated to rooting out corruption and fighting against the political machine's stranglehold on New York City. With the information provided by investigative journalists and the support of the outraged public, the Committee of Seventy tirelessly gathered evidence and pushed for legal action against Tweed and his corrupt associates. The group's relentless efforts eventually led to Tweed's arrest, trial, and subsequent conviction for embezzlement in 1873, which marked the end of his political career and sent a powerful message about the consequences of abusing power for personal gain.

Though justice eventually won, it was not without cost. The tyranny of Tweed's political corruption squandered tens of millions of taxpayer dollars and actively denied American citizens the integrity of their electoral system. The episode is a stark reminder that eternal vigilance is critical to preserving and promoting the integrity of our elections.

Voting Corruption in the 1876 Election: A Dark Chapter in American Democracy

The 1876 U.S. presidential election stands as a significant moment in American history, marred by allegations of widespread voting corruption. As the nation grappled with the aftermath of the Civil War and the pursuit of racial equality, the electoral process became a battleground for power and control. The 1876 election witnessed widespread of misconduct and manipulation that cast a dark shadow over American democracy, undermining the principles of fairness and integrity.

Voter intimidation and suppression emerged as prominent issues during the 1876 election, particularly in the Southern states. African Americans, who had recently gained the right to vote through the 15th Amendment, faced relentless threats and violence aimed at suppressing their political participation. White supremacist groups, such as the Ku Klux Klan, utilized fear tactics to discourage African Americans from exercising their right to vote. This systematic intimidation undermined the democratic process, preventing marginalized communities from having their voices heard.

Another significant aspect of voting corruption in the 1876 election was the prevalence of fraudulent ballot counting. Unscrupulous individuals manipulated the electoral process by altering or discarding ballots, creating confusion among voters, and misrepresenting the true outcome of the election. Instances of ballot box stuffing, tampering, and deliberate miscounting of votes were reported in various states, raising doubts about the fairness and integrity of the electoral process.

Partisan control over election boards added yet another layer of corruption to the 1876 election. Political parties exerted significant influence over the voting process, manipulating results in their favor. Partisan officials appointed to key positions used their power to disqualify opposition voters, fabricate results, and skew favor to their preferred candidates. This partisan control compromised the objectivity and impartiality necessary for a fair and democratic election.

The suppression of African American votes was a deliberate tactic employed during the 1876 election. Poll taxes, literacy tests, and other discriminatory measures were used to disenfranchise Black voters, particularly in the Southern states. Jim Crow laws and systemic racism perpetuated the notion of ethnic separation, denying African Americans their rightful participation in the democratic process. These suppressive tactics undermined the principles of equality and fairness in elections.

The selection of electors, who played a crucial role in the electoral college system, was not immune to corruption in the 1876 election. Instances of bribery, political maneuvering, and coercion were reported, with electors being swayed or pressured into casting their votes for specific candidates, disregarding the will of the voters they were meant to represent. The manipulation of electors eroded the democratic principle of "one person, one vote" and eroded public trust in the electoral system.

The corrupt practices and disputed results of the 1876 election led to a political crisis that shook the nation. To resolve the deadlock, a compromise was reached in Congress, known as the Compromise of 1877. While the compromise aimed to restore stability, it came at a great cost. Reconstruction efforts in the South were halted, and federal oversight was withdrawn, allowing Southern states to implement discriminatory laws that suppressed Black political power for decades. This compromise perpetuated racial inequality and hindered progress toward true democratic inclusion.

The voting corruption that plagued the 1876 election revealed significant challenges to American democracy. The widespread voter intimidation, fraudulent ballot counting, partisan control, suppression of African American votes, and compromised electors undermined the core principles of fairness, equality, and representation. Lessons from this dark chapter called for efforts to ensure transparency, integrity, and accessibility in the electoral process, safeguarding the democratic ideals upon which the nation was founded. Of course, these same efforts must be ongoing from one generation to the next. It is by addressing and rectifying the mistakes of the past that we strive toward a more just democratic future. Fortunately, America has corrected many of those wrongs, and the right of all citizens to vote has been upheld and maintained. But that is the point. As we have done in the past we must continue to identify problems within our election processes, fix the problems, punish fraudulent actors, and uphold election integrity as a sacred trust.

The 1982 Illinois General Election

While there are many documented cases of electoral irregularity in America's history, many activists like to pretend such instances are vestiges of a distant past and that modern elections don't suffer under the weight of doubt and corruption as previous ones did. Sadly, the integrity of our elections has been compromised more than once in the modern era.

In 1982, the nation endured one of the most corrupt elections in history. The 1982 Illinois gubernatorial election saw Republican Governor James R. Thompson seeking re-election against former Democratic U.S. Senator Adlai E. Stevenson III. Thompson won the "hotly contested" race by only 5,074 votes. This was the slimmest margin of victory in statewide history.

This result struck many as odd, considering the incumbent Thompson had a significant lead in the polls going into election day. In fact, some polling had Thompson up by as much as 15 points. Specifically, Stevenson won the city of Chicago by a generous margin, while losing the rest of the state by over 60 percent.

Curious reporters at the *Chicago Tribune* decided to look a little closer. According to an excellent report by Hans von Spakovsky, a senior legal fellow at the Heritage Foundation:

> *The* Chicago Tribune *discovered that the supposed home address of three voters in the 17th Precinct of the 27th Ward was a vacant lot. The paper also discovered that votes had been cast for seven residents of a nursing home who denied having vote—their signatures on the ballot applications were all forgeries. In fact, one resident had no fingers or thumbs with which to write a signature. The fraud was so blatant that the resident without fingers or thumbs "was counted as having voted twice by the end of the day." Not surprisingly, Stevenson easily won the 17th Precinct, by a margin of 282 to 30.[2]*

The reporting led to a federal grand jury investigation that upended the entire Chicago electoral system.

How to Move Forward

Some activists believe that bringing all elections under federal regulations, or "nationalizing" our electoral system, will ameliorate concerns of corruption. Democrats very effectively used the Covid-19 pandemic to increase the federal government's role in these local elections. Yet, the more we centralize elections, the more chaos we create. In every instance, a bloated bureaucracy creates fertile ground for corruption to proliferate.

Article I, Section 4, Clause 1, of the U.S. Constitution declares, "The Times, Places and Manner of holding Elections for Senators and Representatives, shall be prescribed in each State by the Legislature thereof; but the Congress may have at any time by Law make or alter such Regulations, except as to the Places of choosing Senators." To be sure, this statement has been the subject of much debate over the years. But now, it is attracting an amplified role of importance, as a calculated movement for the federal government to seize all aspects of elections is fully underway. And make no mistake, the battle is intense, and the stakes are high. In fact, it is this portion of the Constitution that gave Democrats the confidence to demand federal involvement in state-run elections during the Covid pandemic. And having gained a degree of success during that time frame, now the attempt for permanent federal involvement has become a major rallying cry, and a battleground that could have lasting impact on the voice of the people and the future of our republic.

The problem is this: the Constitution clearly establishes the various state legislatures' jurisdiction over the election laws and processes within their states. But the Constitution also provides Congress the ability to regulate the states and thereby potentially overrule their election laws. This deliberation about election control is rapidly becoming a major concern as the polarization of American politics expands, as is the case today. The need for clarity amid intense debate is essential. We must gain perspective as to the meaning of the Constitution's elections clause and how it should be applied within a vigorously charged political environment.

To do so, it is important to try and grasp the intent of the Constitution's writers. There is no doubt, the Founders most certainly wanted the federal government uninvolved and detached from elections as much as possible and for obvious reasons. Congressional input could lead to dangerous and corrupt outcomes. For example, in his *Commentaries on the Constitution of the United States*, Justice Joseph Story wrote:

> *Congress might prescribe the times of election so unreasonably, as to prevent the attendance of electors; or the place at so inconvenient a distance from the body of the electors, as to prevent a due exercise of the right of choice. And Congress might contrive the manner of holding elections, to exclude all but their own favorites from office. They might modify the right of election as they please; they might regulate the number of votes by the quantity of property, without involving any repugnancy to the Constitution.[3]*

And other issues needed to be considered, such as foreign or domestic interference. For instance, if elections were centralized and controlled by the federal government, then the potential for foreign nations or other rogues to use bribery or additional malicious behavior to influence election results would be a greater risk. However, with elections decentralized and regulated to the various states, the prospect of foreign or domestic interference was greatly reduced by virtue of the enormous difficulty of bribing multiple state legislatures as opposed to a centralized locale. Perhaps Charles Pinckney, a constitutional convention delegate from South Carolina, described the sentiments best when he said, "Great care was used to provide for the election of the president of the United States independently of Congress; to take the business as far as possible out of their hands."[4]

So why then does the Constitution refer to Congress as theoretically having a role in amending elections laws, after declaring it to be a state issue? In Federalist No. 59, Alexander Hamilton took the position that only under "extraordinary circumstances" might it be necessary for Congress to get involved. He suggested a possible scenario in which the safety of the U.S. government might be at risk.[5] That suggestion leaves much to the imagination, but it was a potential circumstance that he viewed could be a legitimate reason for congressional involvement. Federal intervention might also be necessary if a state legislature acted so grievously to deny the election "voice" of the people from being accurately heard. Undoubtedly, the concept of "extraordinary circumstances" could be contemplated a thousand different ways, but the point is, whatever the specific situation, it was generally accepted by the Founders that Congress would only get involved with election matters, which were delegated to the states, if dire circumstances demanded such action. Otherwise, the Framers seemed to clearly recognize the dangers of having elections centralized within the purview of the federal government. This historical context must be brought into the current atmosphere on Capitol Hill.

With all the controversies surrounding elections that have occurred over recent years, many members of Congress, particularly within the Democratic Party, believe "extraordinary circumstances" have currently risen to the level that would now justify federal election control, even at the expense of overriding state jurisdiction. I have personally witnessed the debates and political uproar. As previously mentioned, I was in the Oversight

Committee hearing when Democrats started demanding a federal takeover of election laws. Using both the pandemic and claims of voter suppression, they pushed their election agenda fervently. Of course, the pandemic is officially over, so they are now left with but one rationalization, weak as it is, for their boisterous demands. And factual data clearly exposes the truth, that assertions of widespread voter suppression are nothing other than propaganda, used to convince the American public that a federal takeover of elections is necessary.

Using Georgia as "Exhibit A" in their argument, voter suppression of minority groups in that state were made to appear as "standard operating procedure." So what was the Democrats' solution to correct the contrived problem? They vigorously claimed that voter ID requirements and the "burden" such laws place upon minority groups, in particular people of color, had to go. Really? There have been many studies about the impact of voter ID requirements upon the electorate, but one published in the *Proceedings of the National Academy of Sciences* in 2023 focused on the claim that voter ID laws benefited Republican candidates and hurt Democratic candidates disproportionately. The study discovered that when they were initially introduced, voter ID laws gave an advantage to Democratic candidates. Although that advantage has zeroed out with time, the major takeaway of the report is the assertion was utterly false. In fact, the U.S. Census Bureau's election survey revealed startling numbers, showing an increase of voter turnout among all races. For example, when comparing 2020 to 2016, Black citizens turned out at 62.2 percent, an increase of over 3 percent from 2016. Asian Americans turned out at almost an 11 percent higher rate, and Hispanic voters increased by more than 6 percent.[6]

Obviously, ID requirements have not been detrimental or suppressive to any demographic.

Nonetheless, the claim of voter suppression and thus the call for federal intervention as postulated in the Constitution have created a political firestorm of enormous potential consequence. Both parties have now entered the debate and are offering solutions. On the one hand, Democrats are pushing two major bills, the Freedom to Vote Act and the John Lewis Voting Rights Advancement Act. Republicans, on the other hand, have introduced the American Confidence in Elections Act, also known as the ACE Act. The differences between the bills expose a major philosophical disagreement and highlight a potential permanent change in American elections, potentially tipping the scales in favor of one group over the other. The battle is indescribably momentous.

Among a host of other mandates, the Freedom to Vote Act would compel states to offer same-day voter registration and require 15 days of early voting. It would establish universal mail-in voting and would create a taxpayer-funded system for House elections. It would also greatly restrict states' ability to draw new election maps, and, dreadfully, it would give the D.C. Court of Appeals, certainly not a court known for unbiased opinions, tremendous authority as the venue for any appeals.[7] And if this were not bad enough, the John Lewis Voting Rights Advancement Act would give the U.S. Department of Justice far-reaching new authority to control state elections, to the extent that some states could be required to attain Department of Justice approval before implementing new election laws.[8] The consequences of allowing this type of federal control over elections could be devastating and possibly destroy election integrity.

By contrast, the American Confidence in Elections Act offered by Republicans "would encourage states to review voter lists, conduct post-election audits, prohibit election officials from sending unrequested absentee ballots and enact checks on voter eligibility. It also ends the Washington, D.C., policy of allowing non-citizens to vote for local offices."[9] The motivation of this bill is to preserve the constitutional directive that states oversee their own elections and not the federal government, while attempting to boost confidence in the election process, something that many Americans have lost.

And to say that Americans are concerned about election integrity is a massive understatement. During the days of June 25 to 27, 2023, Rasmussen Reports polled a cross-section of the American voters on the issue of confidence in our election system. The questions asked were not vague, but straightforward and clear. First, "How concerned are you that the outcome of the 2024 presidential election will be affected by cheating?" A stunning 66 percent expressed concern, with 40 percent being "very concerned" and 26 percent "somewhat concerned." Only 32 percent said they were either "not very concerned" or "not at all concerned." Ponder what this question disclosed: two out of three American voters believe cheating will be a major factor in our next presidential election! This is horrifying to consider. Although there have been specific incidents of problems in the past, overall, the "institution" surrounding our elections has generally been considered secure and accurate. Nowadays, it is wrought with problems and skeptical voters. What is even more attention-grabbing is how the results broke down across party lines. As one might expect, Republicans expressed the most anxiety, with 54 percent "Very concerned" and 26 percent "Somewhat concerned," encompassing 80 percent of Republicans who are troubled and concerned that fraudulence in the upcoming presidential election will be a serious problem. But lack of confidence was not expressed by only Republicans. Sixty-four percent of independent voters believe the presidential election will be subjected to shameful activity, 37 percent being very concerned and 27 percent somewhat concerned. And perhaps the most shocking facet of this poll came from Democrats. Fifty-five percent of Democrats are fretful about the upcoming election, with 29 percent being very concerned and 26 percent being somewhat concerned. These are shocking statistics.

The second question was equally informative and disturbing. "Do you agree or disagree: There is no way Joe Biden got 81 million votes in the 2020 election." A stunning 49 percent nationwide either "strongly" or "somewhat" agreed with that statement, while only 44 percent disagreed, correspondingly. Again, the breakdown across party lines was largely unexpected. Republicans, by a margin of 72 percent, agreed with the statement either strongly (54 percent) or somewhat (18 percent). Independents were 45 percent in agreement with the statement, 27 percent strongly, and 18 percent somewhat. But again, most revealing were Democrats, 31 percent of whom agreed with the statement, 19 percent strongly, and 12 percent somewhat.[10] Imagine, nearly one-third of Democrats do not believe Joe Biden received 81 million votes! What does this poll reveal about overall confidence in our system?

To begin with, this poll reveals that election integrity is still a major concern to Americans. In fact, anyone who does not recognize this as an election issue in and of itself is not facing reality. Regardless of opinions one might have regarding

President Trump, he has unquestionably tapped into a major concern with the American people when he has talked about fair elections. Fraud-free elections are something the American people cherish, and they are something they deserve.[11] Election integrity cannot be swept under the rug as though it were a subject of the past. No! It is a current issue that ranks high in the minds of American voters. At a minimum, the Rasmussen poll demonstrates that Americans have extremely serious trepidations about the fairness and accuracy of elections! Let's face it, if voters are not confident that their vote is secure and accurately counted, many of them will eventually cease to vote altogether. And for those who do vote, every election outcome will be regarded with an eye of suspicion. There will be a never-ending saga of lawsuits and disputes every election cycle, resulting in disparagement toward those who won. This is inexcusable.

So without trying to sound redundant, the solution is conceptually easy to resolve: simply secure elections at all costs. And I hope you understand the harsh reality: This cannot be done if elections are centralized and controlled by the federal government. Constitutionally, it is the responsibility of the state legislatures to oversee and guarantee secure election procedures, and to strongly hold accountable anyone who might attempt to circumvent the laws. From my eight years in Congress and from decades of sheer observation, I have come to realize that once the federal government gets a foot in the door, it is virtually impossible to remove the monster. Control of any kind is never released easily, and that is especially true regarding government control. If the Democrats succeed in federalizing elections, we will never be able to return that responsibility back to the states and the people. If elections are to be secured, and if there is any hope of rebuilding confidence in the system, the administration of elections and oversight thereof must be handled on the state level.

10

Election Interference by Other Means

You shall not steal; you shall not deal falsely; you shall not lie to one another.

—LEVITICUS 19:11

You can easily judge the character of a man by how he treats those who can do nothing for him.

—JOHANN WOLFGANG VON GOETHE

O BVIOUSLY, IT IS IMPOSSIBLE to comprehensively address every detail concerning election integrity. Attempting to do so has not been my purpose. Rather, the intent of this book has been to provide a high-level look at some of the essential elements that must be present if elections are to be secure. And above all the specific policies and safeguards that should be in place, the most fundamental component for election security is integrity. That objective must be the primary emphasis. Without integrity, elections cannot be secure. Without integrity, neither the government nor any other sector of our society can long avoid corruption and abusive behavior. Indeed, integrity is essential for any civil society. And in my feeble attempt to illuminate truth, this book has but touched the surface. Like dipping a thimble into the ocean, it is impossible to fully address such a massive topic within the few pages of a single volume. But that fact does not diminish reality. One of the most vital underpinnings that built America's greatness is moral character. And to that end we must return.

With that in mind, there is another aspect of integrity (or the lack thereof) that is seldom associated with elections but has increasingly developed into a major problem. Most of you will remember the chilling strategic statement from President Obama's former chief of staff, Rahm Emanuel, when he said, "You never want a serious crisis to go to waste and what I mean by that, it's an opportunity to do things that you think you could not do before."[1] That comment was stunning for many to hear. It made clear the saying, "The ends justify the means" so far as advancing a political agenda is concerned. Let's be honest, a "crisis" is a dreadful occurrence and involves suffering. But to Rahm Emanuel and many of his allies, the fact of suffering among people is secondary to political advancement. His opinion is to take far-reaching advantage of the crisis first, deal with the suffering later. What a disturbing perspective. But this scheme was embraced by the Democratic party and set into motion a crusade that, with time, bypassed legislators for the purpose of advancing a political agenda. And of course, anything that bypasses elected representatives also bypasses the voters and thus impacts elections and the "will of the people." How can they get away with this? It is a simple tactic. If an emergency can be declared, then the executive branch is granted "emergency powers" whereby the legislators can be temporarily circumvented. By so doing, any idea or policy can be authorized through the executive branch, despite having no ability in and of itself to establish laws. Emergency powers alter the normal operating procedures. What could otherwise not be accomplished through the standard legislative process can be done through the granted authority provided by an "emergency." This is the scheme to which Rahm Emanuel refers.

Of course, emergency powers are necessary when a genuine emergency occurs. By design, such declarations help bolster resources and speed up medical or other basic actions for those in need. Things like hurricanes, wildfires, earthquakes, and other natural disasters are common reasons for an emergency declaration. Obviously, this provision is intended to help in times of real crisis. Unfortunately, it can also be abused. When an "emergency" is declared but the real motive behind the pronouncement is to use otherwise unauthorized power to achieve a political goal, that is an abuse of power, pure and simple.

The fact that emergency declarations can be abused is becoming more normalized and, in fact, it's become a blueprint for political expediency. I exhort you, whenever you hear a government leader use the words, "state of emergency," ask yourself, "Is there a legitimate crisis or is this declaration intended to drive a political agenda?" We have already discussed the Covid pandemic rather extensively, but it was a good example of emergency powers being abused. During that crisis, we saw many draconian measures from federal, state, and local governments, such as mask mandates, household lockdowns, forced closures of "nonessential" businesses, vaccine mandates, and a host of other requirements that otherwise could never have been mandated upon the American people. We saw Democrats treat Covid stimulus packages as a power grab to push Democratic priorities and agendas, much of which had absolutely nothing to do with the pandemic. Senator Ted Cruz (R-TX) raised this concern after observing certain programs being pushed during Covid. "Because all the people out of jobs . . . Democrats are . . . what are they pushing for? Changing the emission standards on airplanes. Mr. President, what . . . do the emission standards on airplanes have to do with thousands of people dying and millions of people out of work in the coronavirus epidemic?"[2] That is a good question, but one that was never answered.

The use of these declarations is currently moving in an even more sinister direction. It seems we are witnessing a "state of emergency" for almost every issue, and like a bad rash, it is happening across the entire nation, and for the purpose of enshrining the woke agenda. For example, in May 2023, North Carolina Governor Roy Cooper (D) declared that "public education in North Carolina is facing a state of emergency." What was the crisis? Republicans in that state were proposing legislation to establish universal school choice, roll back woke ideology, make the state board of education accountable, and raise teachers' salaries by a smaller amount than Cooper wanted. Do these pieces of proposed legislation constitute a "state of emergency"? Of course not! The real factor at work was, under North Carolina law, during a state of emergency the governor has "additional powers . . . to utilize all available State resources as reasonably necessary to cope with an emergency . . . ."[3] Imagine, Governor Cooper declares a "state of emergency" over school choice proposals. Really? The truth is that he was attempting to use executive authority that was granted within the context of an emergency to silence attempts to thwart his push for a woke agenda. This is a disgusting abuse of power.

For a long time, President Biden stopped short of declaring a "national emergency" over environmental concerns, despite many within his party calling on him to do so. But he said in an interview that aired in August 2023 on The Weather Channel that he had already made the declaration, practically speaking.

Reporter: "Are you prepared to declare a national emergency with respect to climate change?"

Biden: "I've already done that . . . We're-we're-we're moving . . . it-it's-it's the existential threat to humanity."[4]

And his push for green energy policies certainly supports his claim. Biden has aggressively attempted to force car manufacturers to build, and consumers to purchase, electric vehicles; he has tried to ban "hideous" emissions contaminators like gas ovens, certain air-conditioners, and incandescent light bulbs, just to name a few. And the way to advance "green" policies is by having an emergency that provides a "green light" to do so, sidestepping the legislators. As I mentioned, this is not just coming from the Biden administration; he is facing pressure from his own party.

For example, in July, one month before his interview with The Weather Channel, nine U.S. senators, including Elizabeth Warren (D-MA) and Bernie Sanders (I-VT), wrote a letter calling on the president to declare a national "climate emergency to unlock the broad powers of the National Emergency Act." They were fully aware that the NEA would allow the Biden administration to "rapidly develop a bold array of rules" to impose on private industry.[5] Stunning! The senators were requesting the president to unequivocally follow the Democratic playbook and not allow a good crisis to go to waste. For that to happen, there must first be a crisis, which is as easy as simply declaring it so. Then, once an "emergency" is declared, he could use his granted powers to override the legislature and the people, and push his radical green agenda, unimpeded.

The administration has also considered the idea of declaring a public health emergency on abortion, which would then allow the Department of Health and Human Services to take a more active role in promoting, subsidizing, and forcing taxpayers to provide abortion pills and abortion-related travel.[6] Again, this would be done by skirting the legislative branch and the voice of the people. And there are a host of other examples that are either currently in play or being considered, such as an emergency declaration for the LGBT community, immigration, and even monkeypox. Let's be clear, emergency proclamations should be reserved only for authentic emergencies, and even then, they should only be used for the good of all, not for the good of one side of the aisle.

Move the Agenda or Win Elections?

During my time in Congress, I came to recognize a philosophical distinction between the way Democrats and Republicans tend to think. Like a coach preparing his ball team for an upcoming game, the two political parties have differing viewpoints as to how the "game" can be won. I became increasingly convinced that Nancy Pelosi awoke every morning with only one thing on her mind, "How can I move our agenda forward today?" It did not matter what barriers or challenges might be present; all she cared about was ways to advance her agenda. Daily, she lived and breathed for that purpose, and she successfully translated that focus to her Democratic conference. Republicans, on the other hand, tended to be more focused on the next election. They believed that more good candidates and more victories on Election Day would help them move the needle forward. And don't get me wrong, we all know that elections have consequences and therefore are extremely important. It is also very true that America needs more quality candidates to run, and in my opinion, we need more of them to win. But at the end of the day, it is not an election that moves the country forward, it's the party or person who moves the agenda. Make no mistake, whoever moves the agenda wins! In fact, winning an election is of little benefit unless upon successful election, the agenda advances. For Republicans to focus so much thought and strategic energy on winning an election is, in my opinion, a fundamental miscalculation. Whatever direction our country takes is determined by the dominant agenda, not by the "team" with the most members.

I could illustrate this truth another way. Suppose I asked you to define elements of the Democrats' agenda. There is no doubt in my mind that you could do so. Everyone knows they support abortion, the LGBT movement, bigger government, climate change, green energy, liberal policies on the southern border, more restrictions on guns, and so on. These items are not merely part of their platform; Democrats push to advance these principles every day. As a result, the Republicans are fighting daily to thwart, eliminate, or lessen the impact of these policies and programs. While the Democrats are on offense every day, pressing their agenda forward, Republicans are on defense trying to stop them. In fact, I believe most people would have great difficulty listing the fundamental elements of the Republicans' platform. Why? Because their agenda is forever being suspended or replaced with the latest urgent attempt to stop the next Democratic proposition from becoming law. Therefore, so many people get frustrated with Republicans; they can rarely advance a conservative ideal while constantly being on defense against an aggressive Democratic Party. Indeed, the one who moves the agenda forward wins.

It is within this context that the issue of emergency powers must be understood. If Democrats really believe (and they do) that moving the agenda is all that matters, then they can doubtlessly appease any concerns regarding the "ends justify the means" viewpoint. If a crisis can accomplish the desired goal, then utilize it. The problems with this approach are numerous but ultimately and most important, it is impossible for this tactic to sustain integrity. Be it by specific design or not, an extreme focus on advancing an agenda will eventually lead to abuse of power and will sacrifice ethical standards. Anything will become acceptable behavior if the only objective is to advance an agenda. "Emergency powers" is a good example. Using this device to solidify political purposes has become an effective tool in recent months. Is it a legal strategy? Probably. I am unaware of any law that would prevent an authorized person from declaring a state of emergency. But is it honorable? Well, that is an entirely different question. Advancing a political mission under the pretense of an emergency is not only deceptive and cruel to those who are impacted by the actual crisis, but using emergency powers in this manner circumvents the legislature and thereby disrespects the voice of the people who elected them. Abusing emergency powers is itself a form of election interference. It all goes back to the question of integrity. We need men and women who will not be driven by political purposes, but by a commitment to doing the right thing, period. Never should "we the people" be viewed as an obstacle. Rather, voters should be viewed as the boss, and public servants should do everything in their power to defend and respect the citizens' voice.

To be clear, the abuse of emergency powers is only one of many examples of how deception is used to manipulate a "crisis" for the purpose of attaining a political objective. For example, consider the "violence crisis" that many cities are experiencing. Although a state of emergency is not always being declared, attempts are being made to score political points on the back of a violent upsurge. Though many refuse to admit it, a major factor for the increase of violent criminal activity can be ascribed to the preceding efforts to defund the police. As we all remember, the attempts to censure police departments were the result of alleged racial brutality among law enforcement nationwide. No doubt, history has revealed far too many instances of racial inequality, and never should police brutality be overlooked. But most law enforcement personnel are upstanding individuals who are serving their communities to maintain law and order. It is foolish to punish all of them due to the bad actions of a few. Doing so has opened a wide door for violent criminal activity to spread, and some politicians are seeking to capitalize on it. The phrase "Two wrongs don't make a right," applies to this circumstance as much as it does to any other. Using the violence crisis for political gain is wrong. Yet, instead of finding more efficient ways to identify and punish individuals who are guilty of violent crimes, the political opportunists seize upon the crisis and attempt to restrict the Second Amendment from

law-abiding citizens. Accusing guns as being the culprit is fool-
ishness. Criminals are the problem, and dealing appropriately
with criminals is the solution. A gun is not the problem, but a
gun in the hands of a criminal is. The Second Amendment is a
safeguard for American citizens, and for politicians to use violent crime as an excuse to restrict it, rather than severely pun-
ishing the perpetrators, is an abusive display of power.

The economic crisis is a similar example. Basic Economics
101 and common sense inform us that it is impossible to stop
inflation or to strengthen economic vulnerabilities by throw-
ing trillions of dollars away or by raising taxes. On the other
hand, it is politically advantageous to act as if you are trying
to save the economy while really advancing political scruples.
Unfortunately, deception and political power are enemies of
good and right. The truth is, behind the economic scene is a
sinister plan to advance woke policies while trying to make the
American public think economic issues are being addressed
and resolved. The Inflation Reduction Act has the correct name
if the intention is to deceive the public. The bill is a climate bill,
and its purpose is to advance radical green energy policy, not to
reduce inflation.[7] Again, while many people are suffering under
the harsh realities of economic inflation and personal calam-
ities, sundry politicians capitalize on the hardship to advance
climate ideologies that they could never accomplish through
normal legislative means. It's an abuse of power.

Many other examples could be referenced. The battle between
Alabama Senator Tommy Tuberville and the Department of
Justice is a classic illustration. Tuberville attempted to stop the
Pentagon from illegally providing abortion access to service-
women in the military through the abortion travel policy.[8] In

the process, punitive allegations were hurled at him that he was depleting military readiness and harming our national security by holding up certain military nominations. Amid the continual attacks and accusations that he endured, the argument eventually shifted from abortions in the military to Senator Tuberville being a threat to military effectiveness. All he did was stand for the rule of law, which prohibits the Pentagon from doing what it was attempting to do apart from legislative approval. Again, political opportunists created the appearance of a military crisis and used that rhetoric to drive a pro-abortion agenda. So many other examples could be addressed. The strategy has really become a common practice.

Having had a front row seat while so many of these battles progressed, I must confess that the fact of what is taking place and the damage it is inflicting upon America is, indeed, disgusting to behold. The entire system seems to have become infected, and the ailment is indicative of a much larger problem: a moral dilemma that is slowly eating away at our foundations. It cannot be overemphasized that integrity on every front is critical. Candidly, each of the aforementioned examples demonstrates a disturbing reality: elections are being interfered with by so-called emergencies. It is disturbing to think how an individual who has been entrusted to represent the people could stoop so low as to view political power as more important than the voice of the populace and the well-being of America. But it is equally disturbing to ponder how any American could quietly sit still and do nothing while political abuses are frequently being used to bypass the will of the people and force agendas upon citizens that they do not support, being pushed by people they did not elect. Then God help us! I'll say it again: Integrity matters.

11

Principles of Secure Elections

*Let your eyes look directly forward, and your gaze be straight
before you. Ponder the path of your feet; then all your ways will
be sure. Do not swerve to the right or to the left; turn your foot
away from evil.*

—PROVERBS 4:25–27

*It takes less time to do a thing right, than it does to explain why
you did it wrong.*

—HENRY WADSWORTH LONGFELLOW

WHEN IT COMES TO securing elections and maintaining
integrity at the most fundamental level of our republic,
several areas should be considered essential. No doubt, the issue
of protected voting can become a complicated discussion, but
frankly, the basics are not nearly as complicated as they are
common sense. And yes, many recommendations could be considered, but because each state holds separate regulations, there

is no way, in this volume, to address the specific modifications that each state should uphold. That said, there are some basic elements that should be accepted across the board, regardless of location. Let's begin with the most basic.

Accurate Voter Files

It should seem obvious that no authentic election confidence can exist without first having secure lists of eligible voters. This notion should be so simple and universally accepted that it would be unnecessary even to mention. However, recent elections have highlighted the calamitous existence of massively outdated and inaccurate voter rolls, in multiple places across the country. That being true, how can we possibly expect to have fair election outcomes? If we are not able to precisely determine who is legally allowed to vote, then it is impossible to emphatically conclude that an election was accurate. Faulty voter rolls are bad enough, but when merged with "mail-in" ballots, we have an ingredient for election disaster. And that brings me to the second point.

Mail-in Ballots

Looking at the voting procedures many states have in place, there are undoubtedly aspects of election protocol that took place under the umbrella of Covid that otherwise would never have been allowed. The practice of mail-in ballots is one such example. My home state of Georgia had never permitted mail-in ballots for anyone unless a request was made along with a legitimate purpose. But because of the pandemic and the fear that it created, everyone on the registered voter list was given a "request" for an absentee ballot. These requests were sent to everyone on the voter file, although Georgia's voter file is known to be grossly inaccurate. I have no doubt that decision resulted in some degree of flawed outcome. My congressional office was inundated with calls from people who either received multiple request forms or who received a form that was addressed to an individual who did not live at the location. It was an absolute catastrophe. In reality, thousands of people received multiple ballot request forms, and frankly, nothing prevented them from potentially voting numerous times. Am I accusing anyone of doing so? Not specifically. But no one can prove to me that it didn't happen, and it probably happened more times than anyone could imagine. To be candid, I feel confident that mail-in ballots were considerably abused, although there is no way of knowing with specificity one way or the other, since we don't know who received them. And that reiterates the initial argument. If elections are expected to be secure, then so must the lists of eligible voters.

To be sure, Georgia was not the only place where significant problems occurred. Again, with Covid being the declared reason, states like Nevada sent mail-in ballots (not request forms) to everyone on their voter file. So the significant problems that took place in Georgia also happened in Nevada, but with actual ballots at peril rather than mere request forms. Imagine, "live" ballots being sent across an entire state where significant problems exist pertaining to the accuracy of voter registration files. This is an enormous potential problem, even if the voter files are relatively accurate. But if the lists are flawed, this error could only absolutely jeopardize the reliability of any election. It is impossible, with live ballots being sent to an inaccurate file, to provide a secure election, which is the responsibility of the government to ensure and deliver. Similar problems took place in Wisconsin. According to research done by Seth Keshel, there are numerous examples of highly unlikely, if not impossible, situations. In Madison, Wisconsin, for instance, there were 312 voters who were registered at a 20-unit apartment building. That comes to 16 adults per unit. Another location had 341 votes in a 15-unit apartment, or 23 adults per unit. Just down the road from that locale was another apartment with 18 units and 376 voters, or 21 per unit. The examples go on and on. Allowing things like this without verification is inexcusable and only magnifies the deplorable condition of election rolls in many states.[1] In fact, in Wisconsin the voter files are so chaotic that their Speaker of the State Assembly, Robin Vos, was forced to acknowledge that the 2020 election in the state was infected by immense and widespread voter fraud.[2]

Suggestions to Clean Voter Files

These are but a few examples of many that could be mentioned. But it is relatively easy to identify problems and to assail states for having sloppy files. The real issue is how to address the problem. Again, we can complicate the issue and generate many excuses as to why voter files cannot be made more accurate or we can attempt to fix the problem. And to remedy the voter files really does not require a great deal of complex actions. Simply stated, the solution for muddled registration files is simple: clean them up. It is naïve to think that with all the resources we have available today, accurate voter files cannot be brought up to date and kept up to date. How can it be that Amazon can keep track of people when they move but government can't? The fact is, government can keep track, it just refuses to do so.

The postal service knows when people move, and in fact, it has both the old addresses and the forwarding addresses of people. Cities, counties, and municipalities know when people move into their areas, as do school districts and local tax assessors. Utility companies know where people live and even credit card companies keep track of transitions. Why cannot a combination of these obvious "tracking" systems that are already in place be used to follow citizens when they move from one place to another? They can!

Why is it unreasonable to require the local coroner's office to forward death certificate information to the state and county of the deceased to have them removed from voter files upon confirmation of death? That should not be a difficult task. Medicare and Social Security are additional agencies that have information on the locations of individuals. These are all commonsense solutions and extremely inexpensive. A host of other avenues can be extremely helpful in determining the whereabouts of people. But someone must exercise the political will to do it. By cleaning registration rolls, the most basic requirement for secure elections will be established, but without purging the files, we are simply playing games. Enough of the fiery rhetoric and political talking points. Without real solutions, all the passionate talk is meaningless.

Legal Voters

Beyond verification of a correct residence for an individual is the question of being a legally registered voter. Again, there is no need to complicate the issue—common sense will suffice. Why would anyone consider it acceptable for an individual to vote in our elections, if he or she is not a citizen or legally qualified to vote? Talk about "election interference"! Voter suppression occurs every time an illegal vote is cast. An illegal vote cancels out a legal vote. Why would anyone who is concerned with fairness and accuracy not demand such behavior to stop? It is never acceptable to cancel out a legal vote! So when it comes to determining an authenticated lawful voter, all that is needed is a commitment to validate and authenticate one's citizenship.

Voter Identification

One of the most basic elements for securing elections is voter identification, and yet by listening to the left-wing mantra, one would think that requiring voter ID is among the apex of discrimination. If that is the case, then discrimination is abundant throughout virtually every aspect of our society and culture. For example, a photo ID is required for basic needs and services, such as opening a bank account, driving a car, getting on an airplane, adopting a pet, renting a motel room, buying a cell phone, applying for food stamps, picking up a prescription, even purchasing nail polish at certain pharmacies, and a host of other things. But somehow, it is discrimination when voting is concerned. Why? I could argue all day long that voting has more significant consequences than any of the above.

Why would anyone be opposed to requiring photo ID before voting? There is only one reason that I can think of: malicious intent. Unless a person intends to cheat or enable another individual to cheat, everyone, regardless of political affiliation, should not only favor photo ID, but they should also demand it from all voters. The well-being of our country rests upon the citizens having free and fair elections. Any compromise thereof is an infringement upon the people's voice, and in fact, an attack against our liberties and democracy. But instead of being looked upon favorably, those of us who understand the importance of photo ID are labeled "racists" or "voter suppressants." Nothing could be further from the truth. In fact, just the opposite is reality. In my opinion, those who do not support photo ID requirements are in favor of allowing voter fraud and oppression against legal voters. And so far as racism is concerned, why is it not considered racist to assume that individuals of a certain skin color are not capable of showing personal identification? Such an assumption is completely biased and in and of itself, utterly racist.

Requiring photo identification is not undemocratic, but to forbid authentication of voters certainly is. Imposing a photo ID verification check should apply to everyone, regardless of their race, color, religion, sex, sexual preference, or any other factor. No one is discriminated against when everyone is mandated to produce the same information. Why is it considered unreasonable to compel an individual to prove who they are prior to voting? It's just common sense.

Secure Ballots

In discussing the topic of voter ID, a parallel issue is often overlooked: ballot security. Just as important as authenticating voters is the matter of authenticating ballots with some sort of anti-counterfeiting technique. Every fair election has the capacity to inspect the final count to ensure accuracy. If the ability to validate election results is not in place, then I believe there is legitimate reason to question the final count. And make no mistake, it is impossible to examine and verify votes if the ballots are not numbered and printed on security paper. If ballots can be easily manipulated or if they are able to be counterfeited, then there can be no assurance of an accurate tally. By the way, the same principle also applies to electronic voting machines (which is another issue altogether). But many of the machines are not auditable. That's unacceptable. Regardless of the method that a state uses for voting, be it by paper ballots or machines, there absolutely must be a transparent system in place to ensure that the voter's intent was correctly recorded. And there must be a technique to block would-be election crooks from modifying the outcome. This is an issue that should be a top priority for every state legislature and insisted upon by citizens. Our country relies upon the voice of the people to establish both the representatives and policies that will govern our lives. Nothing should ever be permitted to infringe upon the people's voice, and every safeguard needed to prevent such a grievous act of altering an election should be in place.

Voting Machines

I am not a computer geek. So my intent here is not to get into the weeds of technology, but simply to state the obvious. When it comes to electronic voting machines, genuine safeguards must be put into practice, otherwise, the machines simply need to be outlawed. Everyone knows that data breaches and cyber-attacks are extremely common and increasing. In fact, some 30,000 websites are hacked every single day.[3] Surely, there is no lack of individuals who claim that voting machines are totally secure. This is particularly true of those who support electronic voting devices. But on the other hand, there is no lack of those who do not trust them. In fact, most people I speak with would probably fall into this category. These people have serious concerns.

Again, the solution to this debate is simple. The responsibility lies with the voting machine industry to prove the security of their equipment. To do so, there must be utter transparency.

I do not know of a single company that sells electronic voting equipment and does not claim their equipment to be secure. Obviously, they could not sell their devices without such an assertion or guarantee. So why should they not be required to prove their claim and unequivocally convince the public of the machine's security? It is not sufficient for these companies to simply receive a contract from a state legislature or other governing authority. They must also convince the voters. Let's be very forthright: If there is nothing to hide and if the equipment is totally secure, then they should present the proof and give it to the public. They should provide a true audit (not a mere recount) after the election, proving the accuracy of the tally. Comparing the printed copy of ballots to the machine count is an obvious place to start. Most voting machines today provide a printed verification of a vote cast and then record the vote electronically. Why is it too much to ask to verify that the electronic tally matches the printed copies? The two tallies should produce identical outcomes.

By whatever means, an honest and transparent analysis of the equipment by all vendors should be required. To do so would either verify the claims of the manufacturer and put to rest accusations from doubters, or it would confirm the concerns of voters and force leaders to produce a safer system. Either way is a win, if election security is the goal.

We all have heard horror stories of these machines being hacked or being programmed to provide irregular tabulations. Although I did not personally experience a problem with a voting machine, as a member of Congress, our office was inundated with complaints and shocking stories from constituents. Many of their concerns were of the same nature as came from the report of Georgia State Senator William Ligon, chair of the Election Law Study Subcommittee, which I referenced earlier. Although his subcommittee did not have time to dive into multiple reports regarding Dominion voting machines, they did hear some alarming testimony that would indicate valid reasons for concern. A portion of the report says:

> *The Subcommittee takes notice of the various publicly reported functions of the machines and hard evidence that the machines can duplicate fraudulent ballots to the point that not even trained personnel can tell the difference between a test ballot and a real ballot. Testimony also suggested that the system responds wirelessly to being reset from an unknown location, as happened with the poll books. The Subcommittee also heard that Dominion machines can be programmed with algorithms that reallocate votes between candidates. In addition, the Dominion machines are programmed to count votes using percentages of whole numbers rather than actual votes, which is a feature incompatible with the actual voting process.*[4]

These are serious issues. If these and other problems regarding electronic voting machines are *not* accurate, then prove it. The sole purpose of an electronic device is to provide an exact duplication of the voter's ballot, and by so doing, to maintain voter confidence. Voters must feel totally confident that when they go to the polls their "one legal vote" will be cast and accurately counted. Without such confidence, many people will stay at home, supposing their ballot will not be counted correctly. That, my friends, is real voter suppression. It seems to me that while trying to generate voter confidence, advocates of electronic voting machines rely heavily on their claims of security but are often lacking when it comes to transparency and proof.

According to Natalia Mittelstadt with Just the News, even some key executives within Dominion Voting Systems have acknowledged serious problems with their technology and have admitted "incorrect results" because of the flaws. As Mittelstadt reported, in a 2018 e-mail from Dominion's director of product strategy and security, Eric Coomer, acknowledged the company's technology was filled with errors by a "*critical* bug leading to INCORRECT results." In 2019, he stated that "our products suck" and that "'[a]lmost all' of Dominion's technological failings were 'due to our complete f---up in installation.'" In another e-mail from 2019, he wrote, "We don't address our weaknesses effectively!" And as recent as a week before the 2020 presidential election, as though waving a white flag of surrender, Coomer stated in an e-mail that "our sh-t is just riddled with bugs."[5] I am fully aware that Fox News lost a huge case with Dominion regarding defamation, so I am confident there is information "behind the scenes" that I am not aware of. Perhaps these devices can be proven to be totally trustworthy. But if the preceding comments are true, and if the statements from Coomer are accurate, then all voters who are forced to use these machines are potential victims, as is America. Voters simply want to be confident in whatever system is used. They deserve full disclosure. And if confidence cannot be ensured, the only obvious solution is to do away with the machines altogether and use paper ballots.

Some will argue that electronic machines are faster and less expensive than paper ballots. Maybe that is true, maybe not. We have seen time and again, that the final tally often takes days and even weeks to complete, regardless of voting machines being used. And further, the cost of these machines, along with the upkeep and operational management, is an expensive arrangement. The long-term cost of using paper ballots is probably comparable, and potentially more affordable. Regardless, I believe most Americans would rather pay a little more for a secure election than to trim the budget and have potential irregularities or fraud.

Handling Ballots

Another essential aspect of secure elections involves the handling of ballots. It would seem obvious that the more hands that are touching ballots or that are involved with the overall process, the more likely are the chance of problems. Because of this, there are significant consequences that could arise with mail-in voting. It is my firm conviction that mail-in voting, except for military and other serious medical reasons, should not be allowed. And I certainly am not alone in this belief. In fact, even in Europe most countries have banned mail-in voting due to fraud.[6] Convenience is often used to argue in favor of mail-in voting, but elections are too important to be relegated to convenience. If "convenience" opens the door to potential anomalies or fraudulent behavior, then it must take a back seat to the greater matter, election security. And let's be honest: Amid routine living, people do thousands of activities in person. They go to a barber shop, they attend sporting events, they eat at restaurants, they attend church, they go to the bank, they shop, they take walks around the neighborhood, they attend funerals, and they do a host of other activities. But when it comes to voting, we act as though the only question that matters is one of convenience. Frankly, that should be the last consideration. First and foremost should be concern for an accurate election.

As is so often the case with government programs, once something begins, it is exceedingly difficult to reverse. As already chronicled, I saw firsthand how Democrats on the Oversight Committee purposefully and with great organized precision insisted on mail-in ballots prior to the pandemic. Through their unified voice and the joint efforts from the mainstream media, various legislatures across the country made changes to their election laws that otherwise would have never been allowed. Georgia was one of them. For example, in 2016, Georgia had 241,519 requests for absentee ballots, compared to 1.78 million in 2020, an increase of seven times.[7] Similar increases took place in multiple states. As a result, today mail-in ballots have become both accepted and expected. Unfortunately, the presence of absentee voting through the mail has produced a host of potential problems, including how absentee ballots are distributed, collected, and counted. As a rule, none of these areas possesses a high level of transparency or accountability.

Distribution of Absentee Ballots

The manner of distribution varies from state to state, but there must be safeguards to determine who receives a ballot. Certain questions should be considered. For example, what kind of identification requirements exist to ascertain the legality of a potential voter prior to him or her receiving an absentee ballot? What will be the method used for the voter to return a ballot? Will people other than the voter be allowed to distribute or collect ballots? There are a host of things to consider. In reference to the way mail-in and absentee ballots are collected, the existence of drop-off boxes, previously unheard of in most states, has become considered a viable option for many. Why? Is it too difficult for a person to walk inside a precinct building and deliver a ballot? If an individual takes the time, energy, and effort to drive or walk to a drop-off box, then why can he or she not drop the ballot in person and confirm the validity of their person? This should be standard operating procedure. "Ballot harvesting," once considered illegal, has now been made lawful in some states, and drop-off boxes have become a significant concern; I will discuss that more with that in a moment. Likewise, there should be protections regarding how these ballots are counted. It appears, on several occasions, that mail-in ballots continue to appear for days and sometimes weeks following an election until seemingly a desired outcome is reached. This is insane.

Ballot Harvesting

On the topic of ballot harvesting, it is unreal that we are even having this discussion. There are so many potential problems that could arise when someone other than the voter is allowed to collect ballots and deposit them. This behavior should be considered a federal crime. Who in their right mind cannot understand that ballot stuffing can lead to catastrophic results and destroy the hope of a fair and accurate election? Again, my home state of Georgia appears to have been the epicenter of illegal ballot harvesting, and much of it was caught on video. An organization, True the Vote, informed Georgia's Secretary of State that it had evidence, including video footage from surveillance cameras placed by counties outside drop boxes and geolocation data for cell phones, of more than 200 questionable activists seen on tape. Both phone records and surveillance video showed that as many as 242 people repeatedly made trips to drop boxes to deliver ballots in what is described as a "mass ballot trafficking operation." The phone data bought by True the Vote overlaid with video suggested these 242 people engaged in a total of 5,662 ballot drops and an average of 23 runs per alleged harvester. The group said many of the alleged drops, more than 40 percent of those observed on tape, occurred between the hours of midnight and 5:00 a.m.[8] The details shown on video have the smell and visual evidence of absolute corruption but to my knowledge, nothing has ever been done to arrest any of these individuals, nor has any of them been held accountable. We will probably never know how many ballots had been manipulated by this operation, but the mere numbers of ballot drops would suggest that the outcome of the election could have been impacted.

Early Voting

Closely related to the issue of mail-in ballots and absentee voting are the overall problems associated with early voting in general. Again, early voting is convenient, but it also creates opportunities for election wrongdoings. For nearly 200 years, the first Tuesday following the first Monday of November has been known as Election Day. The word "day" is significant. Had the original intent of election policy been focused on convenience, our forefathers would have created an extended period so that people could easily get to the ballot box. Obviously, it was more difficult for people to travel in the 1800s than it is today. Some would have had to walk or travel by horse for long distances. Had a reason ever existed in our nation's history for "convenience" within the context of voting, it would have been during those formative years. But they did not consign voting to convenience. Rather, security was their utmost concern. They were firmly aware that a single day provided the safest means by which elections could be held, not offering an extended period for the sake of accessibility. The more time involved, the greater potential for fraudulent activity. Times have certainly changed the way people think, and today, early voting has been embraced and fully accepted by many people, as have the consequences that are associated with it.

Although early voting has gained popularity in recent years, it was not originally introduced for the sake of convenience. Although some were probably decrying the innovative concept, as a rule no one ever imagined that millions would exploit early voting for personal comfort and thereby neglect election *day* altogether. Let's be clear: Early voting was primarily introduced to accommodate authentic cases of hardship, such as childbirth, medical dilemmas, or being out of the country. But today, it has mutated into a season for individual preference rather than an outlet for emergencies. No-excuse early voting has become a rampant problem and has opened the door for unintended consequences. According to Seth Keshel, in Texas, about 90 percent voted early in 2020.[9] Those numbers are staggering, and the practice is rising nationally. According to Mike Schneider with the Associated Press, in 2022 almost half of all voters in the midterm elections did so before Election Day, either by the mail or early voting. This is the most ever, with the only exception being the 2020 presidential election, which took place at the height of the pandemic.[10] The rise in early voting, in whatever manner it takes place, is a disturbing development because it complicates the process, and provides unnecessary time and opportunity for wrongdoing to occur. Yes, there will always be emergencies, and for those situations, early voting should be allowed. But apart from the inevitability of individual crises, the custom of early voting for everyone should probably be eliminated.

Election Law Enforcement

I am sure that others have also prepared lists of measures they consider indispensable for secure elections. Frankly, I could also continue offering additional suggestions. However, my intent is not to be exhaustive but rather to be reasonable and present fundamental ideas that should be accepted across party lines. Allow me to conclude by offering one more proposition. This is something that I talked about on the campaign trail over and over. Every state has laws that oversee the process of elections within their given state. But ultimately, what good are laws if they are not enforced? Further, and perhaps more important, what good are laws if people who violate the laws are not prosecuted and punished for doing so? And when it comes to the issue of elections, violators of election laws are literally attacking our republic form of government and democracy. This should never be tolerated.

Part of the problem is how the rule of law has been significantly harmed and diminished throughout the United States. Heretofore, America has been a place where the rule of law stood tall and unbiased. Lady Liberty wore a blindfold, and for the most part, everyone was treated equally, regardless of political affiliation, economic status, or ethnicity. But today, things seem to have changed drastically. We are witnessing the politicization and development of a two-tiered legal system. It is greatly alarming to see how readily and frequently conservatives are denounced, while ostensibly, those who break the law but are supporters of a particular political agenda are overlooked. Seemingly, they get a pass. At the same time, the "cancel culture" not only opposes but purposefully seeks to silence anyone who does not go along with the left-wing message. I realize that not everyone shares or acknowledges my concerns. I would also venture to say that those who are not alarmed are more than likely sympathetic to the Left. Far and away, the vast majority of people I speak with are deeply concerned with the weaponization of government and its unwillingness to tolerate an opposing political or moral viewpoint. And nowadays, the problem is manifesting itself beyond government. Many banks are refusing to do business with conservative organizations, while academic institutions and schools are shutting down parents or students who do not go along with a particular ideology, and people in the workplace are being forced to embrace certain views or suffer the consequences.

My point in all of this is not to get away from the topic at hand but to expose the reality and depth of a greater problem. As we discuss the importance of election integrity, we must also highlight the importance of the rule of law. The law must apply to everyone and should never be used as a tool to coerce people to a certain viewpoint. To be honest, I would suppose most people agree with my opinion. No doubt, there are some antiquated laws on the books and some other laws that perhaps do not make much sense. But generally, laws, as put into place by our representatives, exist for the common good. As such, a civilized society generally understands that those who violate the law should be punished. The existence of punishment is not only a means of correcting the wayward but is also a deterrent to other people who might be so inclined. It helps protect our national commitment to liberty.

Consequences for Violating the Law

Within this dialogue enters the concern about election integrity. Just as we cannot ignore the importance and sacredness of elections, neither can we negate the responsibility that we have as a society to punish those who disobey the law. There absolutely must be serious consequences for those who undermine our elections. If there are not strict penalties for breaking election laws, not only will the corruption continue, but it will also worsen. Further, if individuals are not prosecuted to the *full extent of the law* rather than receiving a mere "slap on the wrist" when they are caught, the wrong will also continue to escalate. There can be no compromise or tolerance when it comes to violating the sacred trust of the American people with elections. Violators must be prosecuted severely.

Invariably, when I talk about prosecuting those who violate the law it should go without saying, laws are of no consequence if they are not enforced. In other words, why have a law if it is not going to be upheld? But today, although we have many laws designed to secure and protect elections, many of them are ignored or not enforced. In many instances, judges or district attorneys refuse to hear cases involving election matters, and perpetrators face no penalty for their criminalities. By so doing, the law itself becomes meaningless. Chuck DeVore, chief national initiatives officer at the Texas Public Policy Foundation, provides an excellent analogy. Suppose you live on a street with a posted speed limit of 25 mph. Many violators of the speed limit pass your house daily. But there has never been a speeding ticket written, because law enforcement does not enforce the speed limit in your part of town. Regardless of multiple lawbreakers who routinely travel past your house at more than 40 mph, one could easily argue that because there has never been a traffic ticket given on your street, then there is clearly no problem with speeding in your neighborhood.[11]

The same is very much true when it comes to election laws. We have heard time and again about the "deniers" of election integrity. These are individuals who have legitimate concerns with what they witnessed within our election process. But because either the judicial system refused to hear a case or because law enforcement refused to implement the law, we are led to believe that there were no quandaries with the election. This is unthinkable, and it also reveals a system of corruption of its own making. Just because a law is not enforced does not mean that the law has not been broken. As a result, people with concerns are labeled "deniers" and a threat to society, while the real issue is a refusal to enforce the law, which, of course, is the duty of those who have been entrusted to maintain law and order. Instead, there must be accountability and transparency. Those who have legitimate concerns must have their voices heard, and for the sake of protecting our republic, both investigations and prosecutions of lawbreakers should take place when election laws are violated. This final point cannot conclude without another reminder regarding the necessity for transparency. Following an election, when we hear the media and others proclaim, "There is no evidence of wrongdoing," we must not let those assertions

occur without confirmation. Those verbal allegations and assertions not only potentially hide reality, but they depict concerned
citizens as being problematic. I know this to be true, even from
personal experience.

We had serious inquiries concerning the outcome of my run
for Georgia's Secretary of State. Every poll that we were aware of
(including our own) predicted a different outcome, and trust me,
we checked the national as well as state pollsters. They all said
the same, "Brad Raffensperger has zero chance of winning." So as
results were coming in on election night, it immediately appeared
as though something was wrong. The exact opposite from what
had been expected was taking place. I recall telling my consultant
within about 45 minutes after results were being posted that it
was over, and we should all go home and go to sleep.

Again, I want to be very clear. I am not making the claim
that my defeat was due to voter fraud—that is something we
will probably never know. And it is a fact that unprecedented
numbers of Democrats crossed over in that election and voted
for Raffensperger. That cross-over vote might explain everything. But again, it might not. Unfortunately, cross-over voting
is legal in Georgia primary elections. What I am trying to com-
municate is that following the election, our campaign sought
for transparency and substantiation of the outcome. All the
polls had pointed to another outcome, and we simply sought
confirmation that no potentially fraudulent activity had taken
place. On every attempt, we were deprived the opportunity for
authentication. At our most basic request, we simply wanted a
few precincts to verify the tally by comparing the final numbers
between the printed ballots and the machine count. We were
not allowed. Why? If there is nothing to hide, then transparency

quells all arguments and suspicions. The lack of openness diminishes voter confidence and escalates the appearance of wrongdoing. In all honesty, I have no regrets about running for Secretary of State, and I have no bitterness regarding the outcome. I sincerely wish Secretary Raffensperger the best, and we have moved on with our lives, and I am at total peace. But transparency with election results is essential. When it does not exist or if it is denied, anxieties and distrust proliferate among the electorate.

So why is it that even among states with Republican majorities, election transparency seems so difficult to obtain? Further, why is it that so many within the judicial branch refuse to hear cases of problematic elections? If you recall, one of the issues that surfaced multiple times was the lack of legal "standing." There were some judges who claimed candidates had no standing, while others claimed the voters lacked merit. And, of course, no case can move forward without someone having standing and claiming to have suffered injuries because of the wrongdoing. When it comes to elections, if the candidate or voters do not have legal standing, then who does? This issue was a serious hurdle in Georgia. After several lawsuits and years of legal battling, the state Supreme Court finally made a pivotal decision in May of 2023. They said:

> Georgia has long recognized that members of a community, whether as citizens, residents, taxpayers, or voters, may be injured when their local government fails to follow the law. Government at all levels has a legal duty to follow the law; a local government owes that legal duty to its citizens, residents, taxpayers, or voters (i.e., community stakeholders), and the

violation of that legal duty constitutes an injury that our case
law has recognized as conferring standing to those community
stakeholders, even if the plaintiffs suffered no individualized
injury.[12]

Voters are injured when elections are not managed properly or when election laws are violated. But not only are voters
harmed, but local communities, individual states, and even the
entire nation suffers. The Supreme Court in Georgia has recognized that truth, and hopefully, this monumental decision will
offer a noteworthy precedent for future cases throughout the
country. Bob Cheeley, counsel for the plaintiffs in the case referenced above, said:

This decision by a three-judge panel of the Georgia Court
of Appeals represents a landmark victory for transparency
and accountability in government. This decision represents
common sense and is the first time in our country's history that
an appeals court has recognized that citizens of a state have
standing to question important governmental functions such as
the manner in which votes are processed and tabulated. . . . This
decision finally puts an end to the arrogance of government
officials who believe that the people are subservient to the
government. Now, government is put where our founders
intended it to be—subservient to the people![13]

All of this goes back to the final point that was made. The
right of the people to vote is a distinct component of America's

reputation and global repute. From her glorious beginnings until now, the voice of the people has been the envy of the world. At all costs, fair elections must be protected. For that to happen, there are certain principles to which we must adhere, as I have set forth in this chapter. But whatever the accepted principles may be, the "exclamation point" behind it all is transparency and verification of the results. This should not only be embraced but in fact be required. No election should go without public authentication and satisfaction. Part of this involves a "no tolerance" attitude toward those who violate the law. Those individuals must face the full wrath and consequences that the law allows. Citizens who are abiding by the law deserve to have violators prosecuted. Only then will potential criminals be discouraged from participating in election devilries, and only then will the prospect of true election security have a chance of being realized.

12

Final Comments

Integrity Matters Most—in All Areas of Life

And as you wish that others would do to you, do so to them.
—LUKE 6:31, THE GOLDEN RULE

Have the courage to say no. Have the courage to face the truth.
Do the right thing because it is right. These are the magic keys
to living your life with integrity.
—W. CLEMENT STONE

As I REFLECT OVER the years of my life, combining my time in Congress and the years of preparation before, I'm struck by the realization that integrity matters, in all areas of life. Please do not misunderstand me, most definitely I am not trying to set myself up as a standard for integrity. The reality is that I am keenly aware of my personal flaws and shortcomings. Nonetheless, having surrendered my life to Christ at the age of 13 and having actively nurtured and developed that relationship over the years, I am aware of the transformation that He has produced. With all my shortcomings and failures, there is no question that I am a better man today than I was 10 years ago, or 20, 30, 50 years ago. I have a deeply abiding and authentic belief in right and wrong, good and evil, and that one day we will all stand before the Almighty and give an account for our lives. These are not merely words to me; I sincerely believe this with every ounce of my being and try to live accordingly.

Unfortunately, one of the biggest complaints and the most frequent judgments people express to me concerning the Washington, D.C., culture is, "It's just a big immoral swamp, filled with self-centered and crooked people." What a horrible description for citizens to possess regarding those who are representing our country. But this attitude is not simply aimed toward representatives in Washington, D.C.; it is the prevailing attitude toward those in local and state governments as well. And the sentiment goes beyond elected officials to include those serving in the judicial branch, the executive branch, and multiple agencies, be it at the federal, state, or local level. Regrettably, these feelings also spill over into the private sector, too. It seems that we have basically become a nation of individuals who are self-absorbed and morally tainted. And worse, it seems as though we have accepted those attributes as the new "normal." It's sad that we have so easily forsaken fundamental principles that form a civil society. Things that once were commonly acknowledged, like the Golden Rule, which says, "Do unto others as you would have them do unto you," have essentially been forgotten or replaced.

When integrity is missing, nothing good can ultimately result, and everyone suffers the consequences. This is especially alarming when it shrouds an entire society, as its destructive influence infects the current as well as future generations. When a culture normalizes or tolerates the lack of morality, it is virtually impossible to reverse. It is for lack of integrity that we are today watching the decay of American society and government, including governmental weaponization against individuals who oppose a left-wing agenda. This same cancer is also responsible for the two-tiered system of justice that is rapidly developing within our judicial branch. There are many current examples of a two-tiered system, but perhaps none more glaring and publicized than the years of pseudo-investigations resulting in two impeachments. It took years, but Special Prosecutor John Durham finally released a report, and he concluded, "Neither U.S. nor the Intelligence Community appears to have possessed any actual evidence of collusion in their holdings at the commencement of the Crossfire Hurricane investigation."[1] Regardless of what you think of former President Donald Trump, it is morally wrong for government officials to fabricate a narrative for political advantage and run with it. Doing so has produced massive acceleration toward the destruction of justice, the weaponization of governmental forces against political enemies, immense division in our country, and the beginning of the end of Lady Justice being blindfolded. Those efforts created a monster out of Donald Trump that did not exist, and it polarized the nation. And unfortunately, this example is but the tip of the iceberg. There are literally thousands of examples that could be cited from every branch of government and every state in the country. Examples that involve both the private sector and government, the religious community as well as the secular. Integrity matters.

I recall reading a portion of an interview with William Bross (1813–1890). He was a highly successful businessman and the copublisher of the *Chicago Tribune*. In the interview, he was asked, "What do you consider essential elements of success for a young man entering upon such a profession as yours?" Bross replied, "Sterling, unflinching integrity in all matters, public and private. Let everyone do his whole duty, both to God and man. Let him follow earnestly the teachings of Scripture and eschew infidelity in all its forms." The reporter followed up with another question about Bross's opinion as to why so many individuals have failed, both in business and professional lives. It should be no surprise that the answer he gave was as relevant then as it remains today. "Want of integrity, careless of the truth, reckless in thought and expression, lack of trust in God, and a disregard for the teachings of His Holy Word, bad company, and bad morals in any of their many phases."[2]

I have had the privilege of speaking to many groups, both in-person and through media over the last several years. One of the main messages that I highlight is my firm conviction that of all the evils America is experiencing, the overriding root problem is spiritual. We cannot fix what ails our country with more pieces of legislation or trillions of more dollars. Now more than ever, we need the good hand of God to navigate us, as a country, through these turbulent times. And one of the reasons why I believe this to be true is because of the obvious lack of integrity at seemingly every level of our society. We are a broken nation because we are a broken people. We are broken on the inside, and that is manifested by outward behavior and attitudes.

It seems that our country has largely forgotten the importance of personal integrity. No doubt, there have been untold numbers of books written about this topic, but as it relates specifically to the issue of elections, there are four areas where integrity is essential. Of course, there is no magic wand to wave over these four areas to make them become a reality. I wish there were! Although each is exceedingly important, the first one is essential. To justifiably necessitate the other three, a national regard for right and wrong must become normal again.

National Integrity

America once possessed a national sense of virtue, but as is often true, with great blessings comes the prospect of many temptations and vices. Amid the years of amazing prosperity and freedoms that the United States has enjoyed, blemishes like self-indulgence, arrogance, and lawlessness found their way into our society. Along the nationalized journey, we lost our moral compass and became both morally stained and internally hollow. And when the communal understanding of morality is blurred, almost anything can be presented and ultimately, accepted as "right." To find solutions to the multiple issues facing our country, including election troubles, there must be a renewed and authentic sense of right and wrong within the people of the United States as a whole. Some would view my appeal as nothing other than an impossible dream of unrealistic optimism. I disagree.

There was a time in America, in fact, for over 200 years, when we were a nation built upon honesty and decency. Although we don't know for sure who made the following quote, it is often attributed to Alexis de Tocqueville, a French political scientist and author who traveled the United States for nine months during the early 1850s: "Not until I went into the churches of America and heard her pulpits flame with righteousness did I understand the greatness and genius of America. America is great because America is good. If America ceases to be good, America will cease to be great." Although de Tocqueville did not make the exact quote, he originated the general idea, and over time his thoughts were reworded, and thereby this quote has been attributed to him. Many U.S. leaders, including Presidents Dwight D. Eisenhower and Ronald Reagan, have repeated it. Regardless of its origins, the statement is true. For the larger part of American history, morality, honesty, decency, respect for the law, and the overall embracing of liberty and freedom have been our foundation. Ideals like these do not happen by chance. These principles are all found in the Bible and have been taught from the founding of our nation until recent decades.

Like many of you, I grew up in an era when most people went to a church or a synagogue every week. I am not trying to imply that everyone was Christian, but as a rule, Judeo-Christian principles were commonly accepted. Out of that national and moral worldview came a wide-ranging expectation for individual and public integrity. There was a national pride associated with honesty and goodness. Unfortunately, the nation quietly sat by while these ideals were gradually being chipped away. From taking the Bible out of schools in the 1960s to removing prayer, we soon found our institutions rewriting history and virtually eliminating God from our nation's past. Then the unconstitutional argument of "separation of church and state" was interpreted contrary to Thomas Jefferson's original Letter to the Danbury Baptists, and the phrase has now become a tool to further remove God from the public square.

Like a "civic cancer," the mistakes and poor decisions of our past, left unchecked and uncorrected, impact the future trajectory of our nation. This brief perspective pinpoints the reason why I stress the importance of spiritual renewal. We can't experience national morality without deeply held spiritual convictions. "Religion" is the underpinning upon which America was built. He was not alone in his opinion, but George Washington, in his Farewell Address, said, "Of all the habits and dispositions which lead to political prosperity, Religion and Morality are indispensable supports." He went on to say, "In vain would that man claim the tribute of Patriotism, who should labor to subvert these great pillars of human happiness, these firmest props of the duties of Men and Citizens. The mere Politician, equally with the pious man, ought to respect and cherish them. A volume could not trace all their connections with private and public felicity."[3] Notice how he used the word "indispensable." In other words, America cannot exist without these two pillars, "religion and morality." The reason? It is impossible to have a limited government without a citizenry who can self-govern their own lives. Without an overarching sense of right and wrong among the people, corruption and societal harm will run rampant. And when that happens, Despotism and government oppression become inevitable. As crime, corruption, broken families, and other social challenges increase, so does the need for government intervention. It is the only entity capable of addressing cultural ills with any definite authority. Thus, the potential of limited government rests entirely upon the public's ability to distinguish between right and wrong. And that can only come from an internal, moral, spiritual compass: religion and morality.

There is tremendous benefit when the prevailing national worldview is one that includes basic values of morality. Again, using the Golden Rule as an example, when the predominant attitude in a society treats other people the same way individuals wish to be treated, everyone benefits and is mutually respected. However, if the Golden Rule and other biblical principles are tossed out, chaos will soon result, and the lack of civility will abound. As it relates to elections, goodness among the electorate is essential. If a society is dominated by integrity, then there would be fewer incidences of election fraud, manipulation, and other attempts to influence election outcomes, and a greater number of candidates who possess integrity would be elected. If the electorate is generally wholesome, they will tend to elect men and women who possess those same attributes, who in return, will provide just laws.

Integrity with Elected Officials

Second, and flowing forth from a mandate of the people, integrity must be required for elected officials who are making laws, and the laws should reflect the obligatory role of protecting and benefiting everyone. Unfortunately, too many legislators today are focused upon political agendas rather than the good of the American people and our constitutional liberties. Having served in the House of Representatives for eight years, it seemed each passing year produced a deeper and more harmful passion for partisan advancement. When the focus is on party politics rather than the overall good of the country, an undoing of our national distinctives is the unavoidable. Admittedly, reversing this dangerous trend is extremely difficult because the "battle lines" have been drawn, and the media continually adds fuel to the political fires. When I say the battle lines have been drawn, I say it with a great sense of alarm.

American politics has always been rather brutal. For centuries, each candidate has attempted to paint the opponent as a horrible person and a dreadful choice for the people. But the tone these days has taken a step beyond political rhetoric. Things seem to be much worse. It used to be that although politicians disagreed on methods, they were in a basic agreement regarding constitutional liberties and the good of the country. I'm no longer convinced that is the case. In fact, I'm not sure the former reality even exists any longer. People used to frequently ask me, "Why can't you all get along?" Sadly, I would respond, "We have two different parties going opposite directions. There are two entirely diverse worldviews driving each side; one leans toward limited government, and the other toward socialism and more government. It is virtually impossible to find common ground within that context." The battle lines are no longer simply between candidates. The atmosphere in Washington has become so partisan that every day consists of a verbal slugfest between the two. Whether it's in a hearing, on the House Floor, or in an interview, both sides are equipped with talking points every day to trash the opposite. They each view the other as an enemy, and thus the battle is real, and it is very intense. Then the media arrives to throw gasoline on the political fire, day after day. As if that were not enough, social media has become a digital drainage where people continuously rant with venomous passion and keep everyone around them politically provoked. Within this environment, politics has become a sharp divide in America.

It is sad to say, but as we have abandoned so many basic values, political gamesmanship has replaced statesmanship. And the "game" often involves corruption, deceit, elitism, money, and power to advance a political agenda, where "the ends justify the means" and our national interests have been largely forsaken. Of course, not all politicians are evil. There are some incredible people serving: men and women who are properly motivated and who live under a well-defined influence of integrity. And thankfully, during my eight years, each election brought a few more of those solid people. But the overarching trend in the current political climate is alarming. The D.C. culture is entrenched with a movement toward tyranny, political power, and loss of freedom for citizens.

The time has become more critical than ever for the people to demand a high level of integrity from their elected officials. This realism personifies both the privilege and the responsibility of voting. We are not designed to be a country led by personal or political motives. Instead, we have a system that rests upon and relies upon the will of the people, as depicted by the individuals they elect to represent them. So if there is a lack of integrity among political officials, it is nothing less than a reflection of a lack of integrity among the people who chose them. The citizens are ultimately responsible for the representatives, and the representatives should be responsible to the people. If we do not have legislators who protect the integrity of elections and safeguard the voice of the people, then they should be replaced. And the urgency of their replacement is rooted in the fact that, if we lose secure elections in the future, then it will become impossible to replace those corrupted officials. If fair elections are lost and the fox is left to guard the henhouse, then elections will not matter, the voice of the people will never be heard again. I will say it again, integrity matters!

Judicial Integrity

The third area where integrity is needed is within the judicial branch of our government. Of course, those who are involved with the judiciary are responsible for interpreting the laws created by the various legislatures. And of course, everyone has a specific lens through which they view life and by which they form opinions. For the most part, people in America are freely allowed to lean upon their worldview to determine their individual behavior. However, when serving within the judiciary, a judge's personal opinions are relatively irrelevant. The sole basis by which decisions are to be made is the law, regardless of personal beliefs. Judgment is to be guided solely in accordance with the dictates of the law. It is never within the jurisdiction of any segment of the judiciary to create or prohibit laws based upon their individual preferences. Therefore, it is safe to say that only a lack of integrity would motivate a judge to exercise judicial fiat to advance political or personal views.

Unfortunately, judicial overreach has become a significant problem throughout our country. As it pertains to elections, Superior Court Judge Robert McBurney is a good example. In essence, he denied "standing" to former U.S. Senator David Perdue in reference to his claims of an unfair election. Perdue, who lost his Senate seat to Jon Ossoff (D), alleged in his lawsuit that "unlawful counterfeit absentee ballots were counted and certified in the General Election." The judge, on the other hand, accused Perdue of "speculation, conjecture, and paranoia—sufficient fodder for talk shows, op-ed pieces, and social media platforms, but far short of what would legally justify a court taking such action."[4] McBurney's comments clearly reveal a personal bias. The case was dismissed. Without allowing Senator Perdue to present his evidence, the case was over. If a candidate does not have standing to present grievances to the court, especially when the election results impacted his or her outcome, then who does have standing? We must have judges and others within the judicial branch who do their duties without bias but with legal integrity.

Executive Integrity

Fourth, the executive branch, who enforces the law, must exercise their duties with high moral character. In similar fashion as the judicial branch, as enforcers of the law the executive branch should never cherry-pick the laws they wish to enforce while ignoring the ones they do not like. Again, the decision is not theirs to make. Their role is simply to enforce the laws that the legislature has created. It is never the right of the executive branch to ignore laws for political or personal reasons. Examples of this are multiple, from laws protecting our southern border being ignored, to certain politicians being held to one standard of the law while others seem to get a pass for wrongdoing. To apply this to elections, numerous laws pertaining to voting security have been ignored or not enforced. Of course, doing so only leads to further violations and disregard of the people's voice, as well as loss of confidence that an individual's vote matters. No doubt, much could be said about these four areas where personal and corporate integrity is essential. But when all is said and done, we must take a serious look at the problems we face and make corrections where we fall short.

The "Out of Control" Must Be Reined In

At some point, simply talking about problems is not enough. Knowledge must translate into action so that election integrity can be perfected and the voice of the people protected. But few people, when discussing election concerns, look outside the box. There is possibly a bigger question that is often over-looked. And if we do not tackle this overlooked factor, the problem could potentially exacerbate an already fragile system. This book has addressed a lack of election integrity from the perspective of obvious problems, such as early voting and lack of voter identification. However, this other problem is very difficult to correct because it lies beyond the direct reach of voters, but it has, nonetheless, played a key role in influencing elections in the recent past. What are we supposed to do with government agencies that are out of control? For example, the Hatch Act limits government employees from engaging in election activities while on "official" time. The U.S. Postal Service has been actively doing so for years, and they are not alone. Many government agencies, most of which operate by federal unions, take tax dollars and allow their members to use "official" time for campaign purposes. In an Oversight Committee hearing, I personally went after the Postal Service for doing this and even presented legislation to stop it, but to my knowledge, nothing ever changed. But the actual corruption is much worse than abusing the Hatch Act during official time. Take the U.S. Federal Bureau of Investigation (FBI) as an example.

The FBI is an agency that has historically earned great fear and respect, and rightfully so. But now it appears to be totally out of control on multiple fronts, including influencing elections. Millions of Americans were suspect when the so-called Russian hoax allegations were being hurled at President Trump and his campaign team. Something did not seem right about it, and in fact, nothing was right. After waiting for over two years, the Durham report finally was released, and the details were horrifying. The FBI either discounted or willfully ignored information that cut against the grain of the left-wing narrative. And although the FBI knew that the story was untrue, they ran with it anyway.

The Durham report not only dealt with President Trump and allegations against him regarding Russian interference with the election, but it also documented two investigations into Hillary Clinton. One involved the Clinton Foundation, and the other considered illegal foreign contributions to the Clinton campaign. Although significant evidence was clearly available through information provided by a confidential source, the agent who handled the case for the FBI told the source to "stay away from all events relating to Clinton's campaign." Why would that order be given? Is Clinton above the law? One would think so. At any rate, in February of 2016, Andrew McCabe, FBI assistant director, shut down the investigation into the Clinton Foundation altogether. After facing negative feedback because of his decision, McCabe walked back that choice, but insisted that his personal approval would be required for any further investigations regarding the Clinton Foundation. It was not long afterward that FBI Director James Comey ordered the New York Field Office to "cease and desist" investigations into the Clinton Foundation. No doubt, both the FBI and Department of Justice (DOJ), in apparent collaboration, made sure that no harmful information regarding Hillary Clinton surfaced prior to the election. So not only did they prevent negative information about Hillary Clinton from being made public, in September of 2016 the CIA sent Clinton's "plan" to the FBI. It was a plan to link Trump with Russia.[5]

Amazingly but not surprisingly, the FBI took Clinton's plan at face value. They neither vetted nor investigated the claims therein. Part of the plan, the Steele dossier, to investigate

Trump's campaign, was also addressed in the report: "No FBI personnel who were interviewed by the Office recalled Crossfire Hurricane personnel taking any action to vet the Clinton Plan intelligence."[6] Nonetheless, director Comey micromanaged Crossfire Hurricane and demanded a FISA warrant. This took place, despite the FBI knowing that such a warrant was dubious at best. In addition, the FBI was essentially trying to influence a key witness, Igor Danchenko, by paying him some $300,000 to be a confidential human source.[7]

The reason for bringing this story up is twofold. First, there was a distinct and troubling contrast in the way Hillary Clinton was treated regarding an FBI investigation versus the way Donald Trump was treated. Apparently, a substantial amount of trustworthy evidence existed with respect to the two Clinton investigations, but both her cases were closed. On the other hand, the allegations against Trump were false but were nonetheless allowed to dominate the news and sway public opinion ahead of the elections.

So again, the question arises: How long are we going to tolerate election tampering? And keep in mind, based on the facts I just mentioned, the problem of election interference does not always rest with the voters, or elected officials, or the judicial branch, or the executive branch. Unbeknownst to most Americans, so much of their electoral process is in the hands of elected and unelected bureaucrats. This morass—commonly known as "The Swamp"—presides over much of the process. These agencies aggressively and knowingly participated to falsify and misrepresent information for the purpose of swaying public opinion prior to an election. So blatant was the scandal that Matt Gaetz, representative from Florida's 1st Congressional

District, declared, "The FBI has now become a disinformation and election interference enterprise."[8] The FBI acted as though they were the only people (elites) capable of determining who should serve as president of the United States. And with that condescending attitude, they sought to disrupt the voice of the people at the ballot box. Concluding, the "risk" of letting voters decide was too great, they did whatever was necessary to control the outcome; after all, they were the "insiders" who thought they knew what was best for the country. They participated in a grossly un-American scheme to inaugurate their choice for president of the United States.

The Durham report highlights the absolute necessity for the FBI and DOJ to be held accountable. Lady Justice must remain blindfolded, but that has not been the case as it relates to Crossfire Hurricane and other cases. It clearly appears as though the DOJ has become a weaponized tool to attack or intimidate political opponents. To correct this out-of-control agency should be an easy decision, but "politics" has become so meshed into the D.C. culture that any true accountability seems unlikely at the current time. But if integrity were the guiding light, all elected leaders would demand that justice be served. Anyone who has violated the trust of the American people by abusing any government position to which they have been entrusted should be punished to the fullest extent allowed under law. The FBI is no exception. This type of injustice and manipulation must not, under any circumstances, be tolerated.

Concluding Remarks

IN CONCLUSION, THE STORIES and insights provided in this book are not presented for the purpose of self-aggrandizement. Frankly, I am keenly aware that I have nothing to boast about. In many ways, my story is no different from countless others. I was blessed to be raised in a family who loved me, and I was raised to fear God, to love people, to work hard, and to do the right thing to the best of my ability. There are a host of others who were raised with a similar foundation. Sometimes, however, one is not fully aware nor capable of grasping a true perspective of their life until looking back with an attitude of thoughtful speculation and meditative contemplation. Only then, in the rearview mirror of life, the undeniable fingerprints of God, other people, and strategic events come into clear view. Only then does clarity reveal how one's life has been shaped by providential circumstances, far beyond personal goal setting or planning. Such is the case with me.

There seem to be a thousand examples as I sit quietly and reflect on my life. But some of the major events that I've mentioned in this book illustrate lessons that I pray will be effectively passed along to you and utilized in transformational ways.

To be honest, I had never seriously considered what I am about to tell you. The following insight was profoundly given to me by a friend who summarized the key turning points of my life. He simply said, "Jody, your life story has consisted of two primary elements. One, you were living a routine life until an injustice surfaced; then, you stood up to face it." In other words, when a cultural or societal problem arose, it seems at most every juncture in my life, I got involved and tried to correct the wrong and make a difference for the good.

Again, I am not alone with this story. America is filled with thousands and thousands of individuals who have gotten involved upon seeing a wrongdoing. But that is the point I want to leave with you. We live in the greatest country in the world. These United States of America are worth fighting for, and unless people take a stand, right now, there is so much that will be lost. And once gone, it will never be restored. America, and the principles that make her great, are ultimately what this book is about. We cannot sit idly by while the foundations of the country are being tampered with and gradually destroyed. It is our duty to pass liberty on to the next generation. To do so, we must get into the arena. We must be present. And yes, even one person can make a difference. Our nation's history is filled with examples of single individuals who made a huge impact. Now is the time. We must be heard, before it is too late.

Martin Niemöller (1892–1984) was an influential German Lutheran pastor during the 1920s and 30s. During those early years, he was sympathetic to Nazism. Over the course of time, however, with the rise of Hitler, he had a change of heart and became a staunch opponent. But by the time he became involved, it was too late. He was silent when his voice should have been heard, and by the time he awakened to reality, his voice was not heard because the "train had already left" the station. He is perhaps most notably remembered for the following quote:

> *First, they came for the socialists, and I did not speak out— because I was not a socialist. Then they came for the trade unionists, and I did not speak out—because I was not a trade unionist. Then they came for the Jews, and I did not speak out—because I was not a Jew. Then they came for me—and there was no one left to speak for me.*[1]

I hope these words resonate. His words apply to America today.

It has always been amazing to me how often freedom-loving Americans win significant battles simply by showing up. When it comes to election integrity, there is perhaps no greater endeavor that is more fundamental for the preservation of our republic. If the voice of the people is heard, and their resolve enacted, both in policy and representation, there is hope for a government "of the people, by the people, and for the people." However, if the security and sacredness of elections are ever taken away, no action by the people can change the course and consequences that will result. So the calling is clear, and the responsibility is undeniable. We cannot simply talk about election security; we must get involved to ensure that it is protected at all costs. I plead with you, jump into the arena!

Notes

Chapter 5

1. https://www.politico.com/news/2020/02/06/democrats-voting-rights
   -2020-111716.
2. https://nypost.com/2020/04/09/democrats-trying-to-use
   -coronavirus-to-rewrite-us-election-law/.
3. https://www.wjbf.com/csra-news/jefferson-county-it-was
   -miscommunication-not-voter-suppression.
4. Ibid.
5. https://archive.thinkprogress.org/georgia-black-voters-matter-bus
   -blocked-from-taking-seniors-to-vote-a3c3e6580c5b/.
6. https://www.snopes.com/fact-check/georgia-black-voters-bus/.
7. https://archive.thinkprogress.org/stacey-abrams-rallies-voters
   -forced-off-black-voters-matters-bus-in-georgia-4f76800b8e22/.

Chapter 6

1. https://www.ajc.com/politics/georgia-made-more-competitive-by
   -1m-new-voters-since-16-election/HILWB73PC5ECNFZMYCA67
   LPRGI/.
2. https://www.breitbart.com/politics/2020/05/12/hillarys-law-firm
   -that-paid-for-dossier-also-recruited-crowdstrike-to-probe-dnc
   -hack/.
3. https://www.breitbart.com/politics/2019/03/26/aaron-klein-hillary
   -funded-dossier-interfered-in-2016-midterm-elections/.
4. https://www.fox5atlanta.com/news/woman-voted-in-presidential
   -race-and-requested-absentee-ballot-using-address-of-georgias
   -election-manager.
5. Press Release, Georgia Secretary of State, Number of Absentee
   Ballots Rejected for Signature Issues in the 2020 Election Increased
   350% from 2018 (n.d.).

6. https://wsj.com/articles/georgias-audit-of-ballot-signatures
-11608161490.

Chapter 7

1. The Chairman's Report of the Election Law Study Subcommittee of the Standing Senate Judiciary Committee, summary of testimony from December 3, 2020, hearing, p. 12.
2. Ibid., p. 12.
3. Ibid., p. 12.
4. https://www.politico.com/news/2020/12/21/trump-house-overturn-election-449787.
5. https://www.cnn.com /2021/06/05/politics/brad-raffensperger-brian-kemp-georgia-republican-convention /index.html.

Chapter 8

1. https://tennesseeencyclopedia.net/entries/battle-of-athens/.
2. https://www.libertarianism.org/articles/battle-athens-obscure-american-revolution.
3. Ibid.
4. https://www.schoolchoices.org/roo/rush.htm.
5. https://conventionofstates.com/news/what-the-founding-fathers-had-to-say-about-voting.
6. *The American Patriot's Bible*, Thomas Nelson Publishers, Dr. Richard Lee, ed., 2009, p. 317.
7. Ibid.
8. Ibid.

Chapter 9

1. https://www.washingtonpost.com/archive/entertainment/books/1990/03/04/the-mystery-of-ballot-box-13/70206359-8543-48e3-9ce2-f3c4fdf6da3d/.
2. https://www.heritage.org/election-integrity/report/where-theres-smoke-theres-fire-100000-stolen-votes-chicago.
3. https://constitution.congress.gov/browse/essay/artI-S4-C1-1/ALDE_00013351/.
4. https://thehill.com/opinion/judiciary/566044-democrats-election-bills-ignore-the-founders-principles/.
5. https://constitution.congress.gov/browse/essay/artI-S4-C1-1/ALDE_00013351/.
6. https://www.heritage.org/election-integrity/report/the-latest-election-data-show-once-again-voter-suppression-claim-just.

7. https://www.washingtontimes.com/news/2023/mar/5/joe-biden
   -vows-new-election-laws-bloody-sunday-spe/.
8. Ibid.
9. https://www.foxnews.com/politics/no-ballot-drop-boxes-congress
   -decide-fate-voting-laws-2024-presidential-election.
10. https://www.newsmax.com/newsfront/poll-joe-biden-2020/2023/06/
    29/id/1125364/.
11. Ibid.

Chapter 10

1. http://youtu.be/_mzcbXi1Tkk?t=3.
2. https://www.c-span.org/video/?470560-1/senate-session.
3. https://washingtonstand.com/commentary/nc-gov-declares-state-of
   -emergency-over-school-choice-bill.
4. https://www.youtube.com/watch?v=Pb-YuhFWCr4.
5. https://www.merkley.senate.gov/wp-content/uploads/imo/media/
   doc/Climate%20Emergency %20Letter_FINAL.pdf.
6. https://washingtonstand.com/news/biden-administration
   -contemplates-declaring-abortion-emergency.
7. https://www.bloomberg.com/news/articles/2022-08-15/us-inflation
   -reduction-act-is-a-climate-bill-by-another-name#xj4y7vzkg.
8. https://www.washingtonexaminer.com/news/senate/tuberville
   -pentagon-appointments-abortion.

Chapter 11

1. https://skeshel.substack.com/p/point-one-to-true-election-integrity.
2. Ibid.
3. https://techjury.net/blog/how-many-cyber-attacks-per-day/.
4. The Chairman's Report of the Election Law Study Subcommittee of
   the Standing Senate Judiciary Committee, *Summary of Testimony
   from December 3, 2020*, p. 3.
5. https://justthenews.com/government/courts-law/dominion
   -employee-admits-fox-news-lawsuit-machines-have-bug-causing
   -incorrect.
6. https://townhall.com/tipsheet/leahbarkoukis/2020/11/09/most
   -developed-countries-ban-mailin-voting-n2579685.
7. https://electionlab.mit.edu/articles/whats-happening-mail-voting
   -georgia.
8. https://justthenews.com/politics-policy/elections/georgia-opens
   -investigation-possible-illegal-ballot-harvesting-2020.

9. https://skeshel.substack.com/p/point-five-to-true-election-integrity.
10. https://ktar.com/story/5490906/almost-half-of-midterm-voters-cast
    -ballots-early-or-by-mail/.
11. https://thefederalist.com/2023/05/16/it-doesnt-matter-how-strong
    -texas-election-laws-are-until-someone-enforces-them/.
12. https://insideradvantage.com/2023/05/12/ga-voters-have-standing
    -in-counterfeit-ballot-case/ .
13. Ibid.

Final Comments

1. Sean Davis @seanmdav Twitter, 3:03 p.m., May 15, 2023.
2. *The American Patriot's Bible*, p. 563.
3. https://www.georgewashington.org/farewell-address.jsp.
4. https://talkingpointsmemo.com/news/georgia-judge-dismisses
    -david-perdue-2020-election-lawsuit.
5. https://technofog.substack.com/p/the-durham-report.
6. Ibid.
7. Ibid.
8. https://www.investmentwatchblog.com/matt-gaetz-the-fbi-has-now
    -become-a-disinformation-and-election-interference-enterprise-
    video/.

Concluding Remarks

1. https://encyclopedia.ushmm.org/content/en/article/martin
    -niemoeller-first-they-came-for-the-socialists.

Acknowledgments

THE AUTHOR WOULD LIKE to extend heartfelt gratitude to many individuals and groups who helped make this work possible. First, the incredible people at Bethlehem First Baptist Church who courageously stood with me against the ACLU in 2002 . . . they represent the "root" from which the details of this book originate. Also the Alliance Defending Freedom (ADF) for allowing me to participate as one of the original 33 pastors who challenged the Johnson Amendment.

Little did we know how that experience would lead me into the national arena.

Thanks to all the amazing people at War Room Strategies, specifically Jordan Chinouth, Kaitlyn Branson, and Mallory Whitfield, for the incredible campaigns you victoriously orchestrated for my congressional success. Thanks to the voters of GA-10 who entrusted me with the noble task of serving them in Washington, D.C., for eight years. To all the members of my staff while in Congress, both in D.C. and in the district of GA-10, you are absolutely the cream of the crop. Dee Dee and I love, respect, and miss you all! To the members of the House

Freedom Caucus, you are my political heroes, and it was the honor of my congressional life to serve alongside each of you.

To Sarah Selip, my congressional communications director, for consistently advising me and getting me in front of the producers and program hosts at Newsmax. I am forever grateful for the platform each of you provided me. To Keith Pfeffer and the outstanding staff at Humanix Books for the guidance, encouragement, and patience you extended me. You deserve a medal. To Andrew Shirley for the ongoing personal assistance, suggestions, editing, and multiple ways that you helped make this book become a reality. Thank you many times over.

And to the single most important person in my life, Dee Dee, my lovely wife and companion, thank you. You have endured so much throughout our journey. Without your support and encouragement, I do not believe this manuscript would have ever been completed. Finally, deepest gratitude to my Lord Jesus Christ. Your enduring love toward me has been so transformational, and I long to be conformed more into Your image to become a better conduit of Your character. Thank You for allowing a "nobody" like me to have a voice beyond my ability. Only You could make something like that happen.

Index

About the Author

Jody Hice was a Republican congressman from the state of Georgia (2015–2023), one of the most aggressive Republicans on the House Oversight Committee, and a vocal defender of election integrity. A founding member of the House Freedom Caucus, Hice served in multiple leadership roles—on the board, as the communications chair, as the host of their podcast, and as a mentor for the newer members. As an evangelical pastor, he was the host of radio's *The Jody Hice Show* and is now a frequent media commentator. Hice is currently Senior Vice President at the Family Research Council and President of FRC Action, a prominent and influential evangelical group in Washington, D.C. and throughout the United States.